WHY
YOU'RE
already A
LEADER

Also by Paul Lloyd Hemphill

How To Win The College Game

WHY YOU'RE *already* A LEADER

Leadership is in your DNA.
Here's Proof in 88 Short Stories from
the Battle of Gettysburg.

Paul Lloyd Hemphill

To one of God's few but better angels,
my wife, Ann Marie

"...we do not know until tried what we are capable of."

From the diary of Sarah Broadhead
Gettysburg resident, July, 1863

"...everyone has in him, slumbering somewhere,
the potencies of noble action, and on due occasion
these are likely to make themselves manifest and effective."

Joshua Lawrence Chamberlain
Gettysburg veteran, from a speech delivered in 1897

Contents

Introduction

Here are eighty-eight short stories from the battle of Gettysburg
to prove that you are already a leader. With proof comes a bonus: you
will read about your own ability to survive and achieve under the most
stressful conditions.

Gettysburg offers a disarmingly simple definition of leadership:
to *influence*. You are influenced by an idea, or you generate an idea that
influences. Your thinking, speaking, or acting influences you or another
person to act, or *not* to act. It is the power of suggestion. It is found in
the behaviors at Gettysburg and in yours. Such behaviors remind us that
influencing demonstrates our human nature. It defines who we are. It is
what we do. This all-encompassing and uncomplicated definition is not
advanced in business or military schools where often leadership is

narrowly defined as a unique blending of personal traits and "leadership elements" to achieve specific results. From this book's perspective, any form of influence achieves a result.

Each story, which is an illustrative exercise in proving our definition, implies a respectful demolition of American iconography, the kind that consecrates leadership with marble statues on village greens. To the contrary, from the battle's 62-year-old George Greene to 15-year-old Tillie Pierce, these individuals had an influence that affected the lives of those they encountered, regardless of how momentary.

Our purpose here is to clearly demonstrate that no matter who you are, leadership is in your DNA. It is never in embryo and is always developed. You are not a leader *potentially*, but a leader *actually*.

Our definition of leadership challenges two troublesome cultural phenomena: first, the powerful urge in American society towards conformity, and second, a trend away from personal responsibility. Ralph Waldo Emerson, whose wounds prevented him from fighting his next battle at Gettysburg, once suggested that we each have genius that expresses itself in our "inner voice." The problem, he adds, is that we want to conform to society's wishes so much that we fail to hear the voice. We are afraid to fail, to stand out, or be different. In this twenty-first century, mediocrity has sanctuary, and all ideas are created equal.

Pop culture, the messenger of consumerism and conformity, preaches "individuality" by buying, wearing, and doing what everyone else does. Emerson's analysis is also illustrated by those who believe themselves to be permanent victims of drug addiction, slavery, or someone else's failures. Cynics no longer give parenting its validation since they claim it takes a village to raise a child. Accordingly, American culture does not recognize nor encourages our individual inner leadership ability. Instead it venerates leadership as a phenomenon outside of ourselves, the exclusive franchise of a select few who possess well-developed skills, or to reflect someone in authority. To the contrary, Peter Block in his 1987 book, *The Empowered Manager*, confirms our view about where you find leadership: "I say, if you want a leader, look in the mirror."

10

From the battle of Gettysburg the definition of leadership as influence mirrors our own behaviors and echoes what Thomas Jefferson called "the omnipotence of an influence." It implies that influence has power, an unrecognized quality we all possess. Each of us is born with this power to say or do something to make ourselves or another person respond. It also reflects a response to that inner voice, qualities that drain significance from the word "follower," and they are demonstrated in every story here. And each story has at least one powerful lesson.

Each lesson comes from experiences of the individuals profiled. Leadership implies followship, and you will see individuals reacting to persons, circumstances, thoughts or ideas that *influence* them to initiate their own actions that influence.

In contemporary terms a mother influences her son with a statement which he follows - favorably or unfavorably. Likewise, the son leads his mother with a reaction that influences her response. The mother thus becomes a follower in her conventional role as a leader, and the son becomes a leader in his natural role as a follower. Roles are inherently fluid, always interchangeable depending on who exercises influence at the moment. A newborn is a most insistent and effective leader: the new and excited mother is ready to respond to her child's every reflex and expression. Leadership is not only stimulus-response, but response-as-stimulus.

From July 1 through July 3, 1863, in a small town in Pennsylvania, individuals demonstrated influence, or what would be interpreted today as leadership skills much in demand in our stress-filled environment: decision-making, planning, setting objectives, imagination, flexibility, motivation, teamwork, persistence, creativity, productivity, and communication.

With our focus on Gettysburg there is no intent to diminish the great deeds performed by equally brave men in other Civil War battles. Yet our view of history here must be nearsighted and distant from the larger view of the war. The shear number of combatants at Gettysburg - approximately 150,000 - eclipses all others because it offers the largest variety of examples to illustrate the great lessons we learn about ourselves.

Each story inspires.

At the beginning of every story the title provides a clue to the subject matter. The title is self-limiting in that it summarizes only one lesson where there may be several. My hope is that you can use any one of the many lessons here to improve your personal or professional life. There is much wisdom in the behaviors described in these pages. They illustrate what we each possess: leadership and our innate ability to succeed.

Ordinary people are extraordinary.

The Gettysburg battle saw more young Americans become heroes in three days than you may find in any other three days of American history. Of the more than fifty thousand casualties produced by this battle, not a single participant was a professional athlete, rock musician, movie star, or TV news anchor. They were not attendees of personal improvement seminars or members of support groups, and few read motivational books or listened to tapes (they did not exist). Still their actions under pressure will inspire you to do the right thing, no matter who you are or how stressful your situation. They will motivate you to act even when you think your actions do not count. They lived simple lives with little or no claim to fame. They were farmers, teachers, carpenters, merchants, blacksmiths, clerks, lawyers, nurses, students, gamblers, and lumbermen. Some went off to war because they were bored at home and looking for adventure. Most did what they felt they had to do because it was a time of great crisis. Their humanity is yours. It illustrates vividly why reading a little history can be remarkably instructive. Human nature, theirs and yours, is on full display here. Short of biography, this book is about you.

Gettysburg reflects the best within you.

In July of 1998, I took my two sons to the battlefields at Gettysburg. Only when we arrived did I reveal my intent in the tone of a father's gentle advisory:

We come to Gettysburg so you can learn about yourself, to learn that you have within you the same courage as the men and boys who died here. You have within you the ability to rise to a level of unimaginable heroism in the defense of something you believe in. You have within you the tenacity to see to the end the accomplishment of a good greater than yourself. You possess the heart to appreciate the joy of success and endure the pain of failure. You can learn from your failures to achieve your dreams. You can trust yourself to do the right thing when you're up against overwhelming odds. You can carry within you, all the days of your life, the great lessons of Gettysburg, that is, you possess extraordinary abilities and talents just waiting to be discovered. But you may not know what they are until you're tested, put under pressure. That's when you'll discover you've got what it takes to overcome obstacles in your quest to achieve your dreams.

This book demonstrates what I told my children. At the same time it abandons the long-established pedestals of our heroes. Giving someone hero status in American culture implies a deficiency of the giver, that he or she is incapable of heroism. The heroic behaviors in this book illustrate what you already possess. Not surprisingly, it took a stressful moment in the killing of thousands of Americans on 9/11 to force this reality to the surface, a spasmodic bursting forth of what Abraham Lincoln called "the better angels of our nature." What we really see in our heroes, or what we fail to recognize, is ourselves. "The hero," observed Henry David Thoreau, "is commonly the simplest and obscurest of men."

How each story was chosen

Individual stories were selected based on two criteria: first, that the story must easily mirror the reader's own natural ability to *influence*; second, that each account contains at least one lesson the reader can use as an instructive signpost along life's way.

What this book omits and why
- Biographical data is too often sparse because of limited availability of historical fact, but when many personal backgrounds were discovered in

my research to be so similar, it was decided that brevity would take precedence over repetition. For example, some twenty officers at Gettysburg grew up in like environments, graduated from West Point, fought in the Seminole or Mexican wars, and subsequently made their decision on which side to fight. Where appropriate, memorable statements by each person, character observations by associates, and a description of their actions will substitute for biography.

• This is not a history book, but a motivational book anchored in a single historical event. It relies entirely on what historians have written for its historical content, in spite of the inevitable errors and controversies they contain. Whenever possible, I depend on several descriptions of a particular incident or person that constitute the *substance* of every story. My purpose is to use the *Gettysburg Lessons*, which follows each story, as snapshot interpretations to help the reader quickly appreciate the story's compelling messages. Therefore, substance and brevity require eliminating the historian's necessary devotion to what must be regarded here as the burden of too many details, such as exact names of fighting units, hour-to-hour battlefield positions, precise command hierarchies, and scholarly debates, which are discussed more appropriately in *history* books, periodicals, or on the internet.

• Historical partisanship is also avoided. I do not judge which army was right or wrong, except to say that favoring one side is equivalent to favoring the heart instead of the soul of the American Civil War. My primary intent is to use what historians have written in common for the purpose of interpreting what I surmise to be significant but simple lessons we can all learn from Gettysburg. The book's non-historical purpose embraces history as its persuasive foundation.

• I chose not to use footnotes at the bottom of each page so that the reader is not diverted from the flow of the message that comes with each story. Information used is adequately credited by listing the sources in a separate bibliography.

• All *Gettysburg Lessons* are purely interpretive on my part. I do not suggest that I have enumerated all the lessons that can be learned from each person portrayed. The reader is encouraged to email me directly at p.hemphill@comcast.net to suggest other Gettysburg participants who could have been included, with additional lessons that can further enhance the book's theme. This book will remain a work in progress as readers contribute their own interpretations for future editions, with appropriate credit to be given. Gettysburg is the grand metaphor of the never-ending discovery of who we are, and this book will act as a catalyst for more discoveries that readers can make for future editions. See *Note to the Reader* at the end of this book.

• Instead of using the words "Confederate," or "Union" to indicate the battlefield allegiance of each person portrayed, I chose each side's respective flags for display at the beginning of each story.

The format

This book is designed to be opened to any page for a quick read in one or five minutes. The book's title is intentionally worded like a headline in a print advertisement, designed to get your attention so you will open the book anywhere and soon discover the title's meaning. The same holds true of the format of each story: headline first, illustration second, and benefits third.

Benefiting from this book

The rich leadership lessons of Gettysburg are showcased here in ways that can help you achieve under pressure while exercising your own influences. For example,

> • an **executive** learns when to get out of the way of an employee;
> • a **student** learns how to avoid failure and experience great success;
> • a **mother** discovers a proven communication technique with her children; and,
> • the cultural issue of **diversity** is reframed to serve a greater purpose.

This book's bonus lies in how to harness your leadership to achieve goals that reduce daily pressures, uncover abilities to succeed, and overcome the most severe tests of the human spirit. How those at

Gettysburg passed their tests speaks volumes. This volume contains stories that prove you already possess what it takes to realize your dreams, and that everyday pressures can ignite the drive to succeed and lead.

Gettysburg provides the following summary or category lessons on how to do more than dodge the bullets of life, more than simply survive, but to excel:

- Create **goals** or a vision that motivates.
- Have **belief** that you can achieve a goal.
- Create a **plan** to reach it.
- Have the **discipline** to persist.
- Seek **help** from reliable sources.
- Constantly **imagine** your success.
- Trust your **instincts** to do the right thing.
- Accept and use your **leadership** ability.
- Recognize **failure** as a motivator.
- **Communicate** clearly.
- Accept **prejudices** as self-limiting.
- Depend on your **values**.

Each of the *Gettysburg Lessons* fits easily into one the above twelve categories, and each lesson is listed in the back of this volume. The lessons learned from Gettysburg provide much of the armor, weaponry, and vehicles you need to drive toward your own success and prove your own leadership abilities, starting now.

Paul Lloyd Hemphill
Norfolk, MA

WHY
YOU'RE
already A
LEADER

The Battle: An Overview

To internalize the title of this book obliges an overview of the historical event that provides its inspiration.

For Gettysburg residents in 1863, America's most famous battle was a massive invasion of terror. It victimized some 2,400 residents who spent three hot and humid days under the most stressful conditions imaginable. The source of fear and panic was the hostile actions of two opposing armies. The rapid relocation of soldiers was so frequent that gaps in each other's defensive lines often presented breath-taking pivotal moments that determined the outcome of the battle. From hour to hour, imminent catastrophe was hanging over each opponent. The most common and desperate field command on each side was to hold positions "at all hazards."

Ferocious battles turned the local pastoral landscape into the country's largest killing ground. Today, parts of this geography of death are marked by ominous-sounding localities: the Slaughter Pen, Bloody Run, The Valley of Death, and Devil's Den. Anything with a roof - homes, barns, churches, warehouses, hotels, and stores - quickly became crude hospitals. Horrific screams from the wounded and dying could be heard in every direction as surgeons amputated arms and legs with contaminated hacksaws. The stench of rotting corpses and animal excrement was everywhere.

Sixty-nine-year-old Gettysburg resident John Burns left his house intent on adding just one more rifle to the Union effort. After being wounded several times, he did what no soldier does on a battlefield: return home at the end of the day. He was a tiny drop of routine in a raging sea of chaos.

In three days, approximately 51,000 soldiers were either killed, wounded, captured or missing. Miraculously, only one resident civilian was killed. For all his vicious behavior towards the enemy, the Civil War soldier did little harm to most civilians. Stories abound of Rebel soldiers at Gettysburg who were respectful and humane towards citizens in their capture. These same citizens, remarked one Rebel soldier, "are very kind considering we came here to kill off their husbands and sons." By modern standards, men fighting on both sides took extraordinary measures to avoid collateral damage while making deliberate surgical strikes in their efforts to kill.

The impulsiveness of a newly promoted Rebel commander and the support of an equally impetuous superior ignited the battle. Their lack of proper planning and careless attitude would hasten a human calamity the likes of which had never been witnessed in recorded American history.

Along with dust, thirst, hunger, and exhausting twenty-to-thirty-mile marches just to reach the battlefields, excessive heat would prove to be too great an adversary for both armies; neither side could fight at peak performance. Days before the battle, one Union commander reported that hundreds of his men had collapsed from sunstroke on a single day's march. Soldiers wore wool clothing in temperatures between seventy-five and ninety degrees. One Rebel veteran remarked that the "vertical rays of the sun seemed like real lances of steel tipped with fire!"

The morning of July 1, 1863 would mark a beginning of the end of the Civil War. The "High Water Mark of the Confederacy" would be the aquatic metaphor forever used to mark the end of a quest for Southern independence. Three days of fighting produced a cruel double irony that would carry providential undertones: the death of an infant nation in its cradle would be localized on *Cemetery* Ridge and be dated on the eve of the 4th of July, the date marking the birth of a new nation, four score and seven years earlier.

Despite the many defeats Confederate General Robert E. Lee was handing the enemy, arithmetic and time were working against him. Previous battles forced a rapid depletion of food, manpower, and talented officers. More daring action was required to change the losing fortunes of victory. Supported by the Confederate cabinet in Richmond, Lee devised one last dramatic invasion plan of the North. The South calculated that victory over a superior foe on northern soil would encourage intervention by foreign nations. The goal was to legitimize the Confederacy once and for all, and a profoundly religious Lee saw Pennsylvania as the Promised Land for Southern sovereignty.

July 1: *The First Day*

Confederate General Johnston Pettigrew marches toward the town the day before and discovers what appears to be a sizeable group of Union cavalry. Remembering Lee's orders not to engage the enemy until the entire Rebel army is massed and ready, he withdraws from a possible fight. A brilliant scholar and author, Pettigrew informs his superior of what he has seen. By his overwhelming eagerness to position himself for a fight, General "Harry" Heth reacts to Pettigrew's assessment with unconvincing disbelief. Desire exceeds his prudence to follow a Lee directive that Pettigrew clearly understands. As a result, the world of Gettysburg explodes and the bloodiest battle of the Civil War begins.

Heth has a case of bad luck when engaging Union General John Buford. Outnumbered but not outsmarted, Buford proceeds to hold off Heth's Rebels until his associate, General John Reynolds, arrives to help repel a strong attack. Reynolds understands that high odds have to be met by high risks. His men are successful for the moment, but Reynolds is killed instantly. Abner Doubleday immediately assumes command. He does a commendable job of managing a difficult line of battle and retreating to a more secure position in order to continue the fight near a cemetery south of town. Regrettably, Doubleday's reputation for being slow to act forces his superior, O.O. Howard, to misjudge his actions and remove him from his command. Discouraged and humiliated by his own leaders, Doubleday leaves the battle a bitter man.

Meanwhile, a young girl is shocked when forced to do what belongs in the domain of adult expectations. She becomes a beacon of hope to the wounded and dying, and learns of qualities within herself that she never knew existed. For teenager Tillie Pierce, cruel moments of stress give rise to a painful but positive self-discovery. She is the youngest example of leadership at its best.

The South is winning on the first day, pushing the Union men back towards the town of Gettysburg. However, it does not come without a high price. Confederate General Robert Rodes, cocky after so many successes, ignores the most basic rule in any confrontation - assessing the strengths and weaknesses of his competitor before attacking. Plus, one of his commanders, Alfred Iverson, sends his troops into a murderous Union ambush. Instead of assuming the responsibility for not leading his men, Iverson condemns the surrender of a few survivors as "disgraceful." Leadership's dark side makes a disturbing debut.

On the first day, Union troops are forced to retreat against superior odds. Valiant efforts are being made to hold their ground. A shell fragment that partially severs his right leg hits the teenage commander of an artillery unit, Bayard Wilkeson. Completing the amputation himself with a pocketknife, Wilkeson demonstrates the meaning of courage in unimaginable pain. Youthful Union General Francis Barlow attempts to rally his men for one more fight, but personal prejudice against his own foreign-born soldiers results in his inability to lead them. Ethnic discrimination leads to disastrous results.

Union forces regroup on high ground south of town. Lee orders Confederate General Richard Ewell to attack the Union position "if practicable." He hesitates to charge the fortified hill that later proved an invaluable position for the Union army. Meanwhile, Ewell stands watching another but untaken hill slip slowly through his fingers as it too becomes occupied and reinforced. He becomes so outnumbered that he prudently moves away from what is now a very dangerous position. His hesitancy is responsible for what may be the greatest missed opportunity in the battle.

Overlooking Gettysburg from his newly fortified perch, Union General O. O. Howard waits for orders from General Meade, commander of the Army of the Potomac, who is some fifteen miles away. With disheartened foreign-born troops under his command, Howard is still able to exercise a cool and firm control in retreating to a much needed hill. The failure of these foreigners is due, in part, to their great contempt for Howard.

As the day progresses, Confederate General James Longstreet concludes that the Union positions are too strong to mount a successful offensive. He suggests taking a defensive position that would require the enemy to attack first, which would force the reversal of strategies of the two armies. Lee disagrees. He believes his invincible army is going to thrash what he refers to as "those people" on the southern end of the Union line. After achieving great results from taking huge risks in previous engagements, Lee has developed a careful plan that he believes, with God's help, will work.

Union General Winfield Scott Hancock takes on the role of head coach of the Union forces. He rallies the beaten players to dig in. From this moment forward, Hancock appears to be everywhere at the right time, correctly assessing the circumstances and communicating the right orders in the most frantic situations. Hancock is a rallying point in full motion.

July 2: *The Second Day*

At the conclusion of the first day's fighting Lee is optimistic. Lee is planning big; Meade is planning small. Lee wants to end the war at Gettysburg; Meade wants to prevent Lee from attacking Baltimore and Washington. Meade will defeat Lee by doing all of the right things. What prevents Meade from concluding the war, becoming the nation's greatest war hero and having the White House as his future address becomes painfully clear: not only do his orders define a goal less than Lee's, but exhausted and hungry troops, a battered command structure, and the lateness of the day make it impossible for him to crush Lee and end the war. Meade's objective, as defined by his orders from Washington, is limited in scope and framed, in his own words, to "driving the last vestiges of the enemy from our soil." In short, Lee works with a vision not constrained by orders, and Meade is constrained by orders without a vision.

The weapon of mass destruction under Meade's command is his capable artillery chief, General Henry Hunt, who knows where and when to position his cannons. Hunt will employ a deceptive maneuver and attempt to spring it at the most opportune moment. But Hunt's seemingly full-proof attempt is dismissed by General Hancock, who has tactical control over that area of the field where Hunt's guns are stationed. Implicit is the confusion of just who commands and controls their own ground of battle, not to mention a lack of integration of separate command strategies.

Lee orders General Longstreet to mount an attack against a Union position located in and around a peach orchard. Bogged down by poor staff work, little or no cavalry, and multiple changes that result in delays, Longstreet takes at least five hours to begin his attack. Lack of Rebel organization buys the Union several hours to reinforce itself. An egomaniacal Union commander, General Dan Sickles, attempts to make an out-of-my-way charge toward his own personal glory.

Contrary to General Meade's intentions, Sickles decides to place his men beyond a strong Union line near the same peach orchard where Longstreet's troops are headed. A gap in the Union line is created. The South attacks forcefully. Sickles's rashness causes him to lose a leg and to suffer thousands of casualties. Other Union generals do what they can to save Sickles from his catastrophe. The high price is the loss of courageous men like George Ward, who hobbles about on a wooden leg with a crutch in one hand and a sword in the other.

Men who have never seen battle before find themselves taking heroic measures. Many are part of Union Captain Bigelow's artillery unit. They manage to stall the Confederate onslaught for a vital thirty minutes, buying their cohorts enough time to close another gap in the Union line. The result goes a long way to prove that in the absence of experience, discipline can help you make the right decisions to achieve desired results.

Confederate General William Barksdale, whose love for a fight is legendary, charges into one of the greatest ironies of Civil War battles: he is defeated by George Willard, the same man he had captured and held prisoner at Harper's Ferry ten months earlier. In the prisoner culture of the Civil War, being excused from the shame of capture was an all-consuming mindset. Willard's triumph and redemption turns into tragedy. Minutes later, hurrying back in the glow of a small victory, he is partially decapitated by an enemy shell.

Hancock sees that the Union stronghold is threatened at a point where only two hundred and sixty-two men from Minnesota are available to engage nearly one thousand charging Southerners. Most of these Union men know that the order to attack means certain death. Forty-two survivors live to tell about their success against impossible odds. It buys Hancock the five crucial minutes he needs for reinforcements to arrive. Like so many other pivotal moments in this great battle, the effect of selflessness makes a difference in a nation's destiny.

The death toll continues to climb in a wheat field. Back and forth goes its possession, and a New Hampshire colonel's timely prediction of his own death comes true. The chilling cries of dying men are everywhere. One Rebel soldier summarizes the day as "hot, hotter, hottest."

On top of a small hill known as Little Round Top stands Union General Gouveneur Warren. Except for a few signalmen, he discovers the hill unoccupied. Realizing the tactical advantage of the hill's immediate occupancy, he sends for support. Another officer, Colonel Strong Vincent, contrary to his standing orders, rushes his own men to the summit and positions them where he believes they will be most effective. His strategy works. A group from Maine, headed by a former college professor, Joshua Lawrence Chamberlain, is ordered to hold the extreme left of the Union line. Chamberlain's men eventually run out of ammunition, but with a move that can only be described as innovative, he succeeds in saving the end of the Union line. He has the help of a young officer, Orpheus Woodward, who makes an ostensibly insignificant move that results in Chamberlain's success.

At the opposite end of the Union position, "Old Pop" George Greene orders his men to put up defenses for a possible attack. The Boy Scout motto, "Be Prepared," has its best example in Greene, and the position known as Culp's Hill remains in Union hands. Sickly Colonel Thomas Kane remains on this hill during the fighting, and demonstrates how getting out of the way of his own men can lead to success at the most pressuring moment.

After an exhaustive forty-eight hours, there are over thirty thousand casualties on both sides combined. Most of the dead, including some three thousand animals, are unburied and, due to embryonic diseases, remain silent killing agents were they lay. During these hot and humid days, the stench is suffocating. The cries of thousands of wounded still on the fields are a cacophony of hopelessness and despair. One soldier later expresses fear of being eaten alive by roaming hogs that are seen tearing at the flesh of the dead. The fortitude of survivors is pushed beyond its limits, leaving each to wonder not *if*, but *when* their turn to die will come. Another day's fighting is still ahead.

July 3: *The Final Day*

General Longstreet tries again to convince General Lee not to attack a strong Union position. In fact, the North is so well situated that one Union commander suggests to Meade that the Rebels "have hammered us into a solid position they cannot whip us out of." In a late night conference the rest of Meade's commanders agree to remain in a defensive posture. Lee assumes that his adversary is too exhausted and demoralized to withstand another attack and wants to hit him at the center of his line on Cemetery Ridge.

Lee is only guessing because the eyes and ears of his army, cavalry commander JEB Stuart, shows up in the middle of the battle intent on impressing his commanding general with captured enemy booty, but his real job is to inform Lee of enemy movements. Lee has come this far without Stuart, up to now depending on the word of a former actor and spy for Longstreet. Lee is listening to the advice of his aides and several generals to construct a plan of attack. The plan includes a physical reference point - a group of trees on a ridge - on the way to an all-important hill, what appears to be his final objective. One Union officer interprets Lee's focus: "The decision of the Rebel commander [Lee] was upon that point; the concentration of artillery was upon that point; the din of battle developed in a column of attack upon that point; the greatest effort...was at that point..." Nevertheless, the implementation of Lee's plan is about to damage his great army.

The day begins after 4:00 a.m., and for the next seven hours of blood-letting, not an inch of ground is gained by either side. During this time, a tragic misunderstanding is unfolding. A verbal order is misinterpreted, and it results in the senseless wounding and death of nearly two hundred and fifty men in less than ten minutes. To obey an order that is understood to mean certain death causes one to ponder the meaning of futility and wasted valor.

The fight for Culp's Hill, the most desperate of the battle, stops around 11:00 a.m. What follows is an eerie silence that speaks eloquently of the anxiety in both armies as the temperature approaches ninety degrees.

Longstreet persists in trying to convince Lee that a frontal attack of nearly thirteen thousand men in an open field will fail. Lee ignores the advice and orders his artillery to commence firing. Earlier, Meade predicts that Lee will strike him at his center. Lee expects Stuart's cavalry to make an effort on this final day, but Stuart fails when he goes up against a strong Union commander like David Gregg.

Commencing at approximately 1 p.m. on July 3, and lasting for more than an hour, more than one hundred and fifty Confederate cannons are blazing with less effect than the Union response. It is discovered after the battle that one sixteen-foot section of rail fence in front of Union troops is marked with eight hundred and thirty-six holes. One Rebel captain said later, "How like hail upon a roof sounded the patter of the enemy's bullets upon that fence!"

The cannons cause a blinding smoke that covers the field. Union General Henry Hunt orders several cannons to the rear in the hope that, despite the smoke, his Confederate adversary, Colonel Alexander, will notice and assume his foe is out of ammunition. The bait is taken. Longstreet receives a message from his artillery commander urging Pickett to move out quickly. General Pickett takes a reluctant nod from Longstreet to begin the attack. Unknown to anyone is the greatest agony that has befallen any commander at Gettysburg. Longstreet must issue what he believes are two horrific orders: make an attack he is convinced will fail, and then follow up with a second charge whose result will repeat the first. A torturous dilemma will force him to make the unthinkable the inevitable, or what becomes enshrined as the most momentous hour in Civil War history: Pickett's Charge.

A defeatist sentiment felt by any number of Rebel soldiers was written by a survivor: "We waited patiently...for the order that would seal our fate." Less than a mile away from Union defenses, about thirteen thousand Confederates form a line that is more than a mile wide. Somberly they march toward their opponent on Cemetery Ridge, causing one Rebel sergeant to remark: "Men prayed on that field that never prayed before." Union soldiers are watching in admiration at what looks like a parade full of pageantry and precision.

Once the Confederates are within range, Union General Hunt beholds a target-rich landscape. Although a rapid depletion of ammunition will frustrate his plan for an effective triangulation of artillery fire, he is able to cripple the Southern advance. Likewise deadly accurate rifle volleys are tearing open huge gaps in the Rebel lines. "Arms, heads, blankets, guns and knapsacks," observed one Union soldier from Ohio, "were thrown and tossed into the clear air." Amazed at the determination of the attackers to keep their lines in order, another was heard to say, "What men are these we slaughter like cattle and still they come at us?"

Southern choreography continues to dissolve into a mass of dismembered bodies. Moreover, outwardly insignificant but sturdy post-and-rail fences planted squarely in the path of the charge depress any momentum the Rebels have left in their final stages of the attack, and they force a disciplined and rushing army to stand virtually still and disorganized, temporary enough to be a generous target. "Where the parallel fences impeded the onward march," observed one Rebel officer, "large numbers were shot down on account of the crowding...and on account of the halt in order to climb the fences." It is perhaps the banality of minor details that these impediments are overlooked in the planning of the attack, only to prove that careful preparation must defer to the stubbornly obvious.

As the remaining Confederates move closer, Union General Hays summons all the enthusiasm he can muster, shouting to his men that soon they "should see some fun!" A low stone wall barely shelters the waiting Union troops. Hays's fellow commander, 28-year-old General Alexander Webb, is taking the brunt of the attack. The Confederates make one stop, fire their own volley, and then begin running toward their target. A Confederate captain turns to take one last look at his dying son on the ground before rejoining the charge. Rebel leader General Lewis Armistead leaps over the wall and yells, "Boys! Give them the cold steel!" With at least two bullets in his body he falls mortally wounded. Ironically his dearest friend from former days, Union General Hancock, also lay wounded not far away. The most heartrending statement of what may be the most stressful moment is made by a Union private, who recalls beckoning a Confederate to surrender: "I tried to save him, but he would not give up, so I had to kill him to save my own life."

Two Union generals are wounded near Lee's main point of attack. The Union line now appears leaderless. What unfolds is a lesson of leadership from the bottom: ordinary soldiers understand and internalize the objective from the top so that they are no longer in need of someone in charge. Observing his fellow soldiers, one Rebel veteran remarked that "every man felt...that he was his own commander." A Yankee private from Minnesota concluded:

> ...we had no more need for a commander for we would now have achieved a victory had we been left without an officer [,] for we could see every movement of the enemy and know how to defend our hills. In short we did the rest of the commanding ourselves.

Stressful circumstances ordain followers to be leaders.

In an era when day-old information is considered up-to-the-minute, the New York Stock Exchange receives news at three o'clock that the fighting of the previous day went well for the North. As a result, the market becomes bullish, and one railroad company's stock goes up one and a quarter points.

Young Union General Webb is having difficulty coordinating his troops to make an effective defense of his position. Reinforcements, who include Private David Hemphill, are rushed to his aid. The Rebels are forced to ditch their valiant effort with over six thousand casualties on the field. With a note of bizarre melodrama, a wounded soldier from North Carolina remarks afterward, "I was dead awhile." Except for one minor cavalry fight, the battle is over.

The date of the battle's conclusion creates a potent metaphor for the inevitability of Northern supremacy: as the dream of a Southern Confederacy departs in shatters, the eighty-seventh anniversary of the Union's birth arrives precisely on schedule.

July 1
The First Day

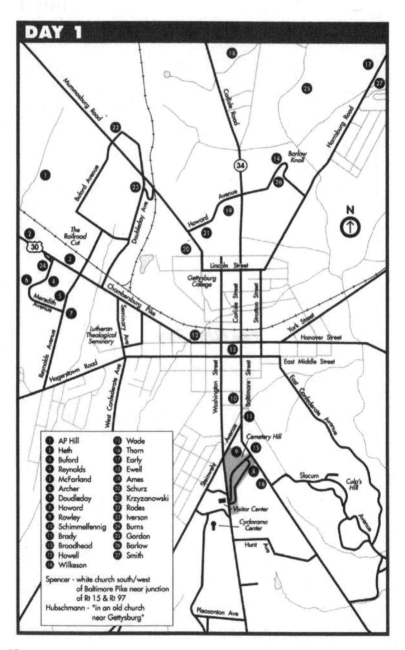

DAY 1

N

1. AP Hill
2. Heth
3. Buford
4. Reynolds
5. McFarland
6. Archer
7. Doudleday
8. Howard
9. Rowley
10. Schimmelfennig
11. Brady
12. Broadhead
13. Howell
14. Wilkeson
15. Wade
16. Thorn
17. Early
18. Ewell
19. Ames
20. Schurz
21. Krzyzanowski
22. Rodes
23. Iverson
24. Burns
25. Gordon
26. Barlow
27. Smith

Spencer - white church south/west of Baltimore Pike near junction of Rt 15 & Rt 97
Hubschmann - "in an old church near Gettysburg"

Use the ASK formula.

A. P. Hill

A. P. Hill's commander, Robert E. Lee, believed that God had a lot to do with the outcome of battles. But God was not in the details for Hill. As an impulsive warrior, Hill was convinced that victory came with a heavy dose of self-confidence. Not a religious man, he was probably superstitious, wearing a red flannel shirt into every battle and keeping a good-luck hambone from his mother in his pocket.

In spite of being ill on the first day of the battle, he was eager for a fight. He loved the thrill of defeating an opponent and the exhilarating feelings that came with victory. He wanted to be in the thick of the battle and again accomplish feats for which he was known in other engagements, like "rescuing" General Lee at the battle of Antietam. Such achievements perhaps validated for Hill an impulsiveness that would wreak havoc later on Lee's plans for an offensive battle.

With his ability to motivate troops who admired him and a reputation for molding the best fighting unit in the Confederate army, Hill was a one-man command team. Although he spearheaded victory for the South on the first day at Gettysburg, he made significant errors in judgment. Prior to the battle he practically dismissed a subordinate officer's warning that there was a group of Yankee cavalry ahead. He considered it a mere "detachment of observation" (He was calling a looming hurricane a gentle breeze) that could not withstand an assault by a large body of Rebel infantry. Without notifying his commander, a hasty Hill ignored signs of the greater danger and allowed one of his commanders to take the initiative that would eventually blow in the storm. As a result, Lee was forced to abandon his plan of concentrating his entire army at Cashtown (eight miles from Gettysburg) that called for preventing the Union army, in Lee's words, "from advancing farther west, and intercepting our communication with Virginia." Hill's impetuosity was history's way to guarantee that the Civil War's greatest battle would never be called the Battle of Cashtown.

On the second day, ordered by Lee to support another commander in an attack and to make certain that his own commanders were following their assignments, Hill was nowhere near the top of his game. With opportunities being lost, it was apparent that illness was trumping command responsibilities.

The third day for Hill was a near repeat of the second. Lee ordered him to be ready as a support force during Pickett's Charge. His participation was never ordered. As a warrior abandoned to the periphery, Hill allowed his artillery to engage in a wasteful use of precious ammunition on a barn, and disallowed its use when it could have been most effective. In short, the talented but sickly Hill contributed little to the Southern effort at Gettysburg.

Gettysburg Lessons

Use the ASK formula.

When immediate problems demand immediate solutions, find people who are willing to help, especially the most enthusiastic like Hill who are eager to prove themselves. They will assist you by the influence of your request. If perfect strangers will take the time and energy to give you travel directions when you are lost, people known to you will come to your rescue. They may be family members, associates, or employees. Always use the ASK formula for success: Ask and you shall receive; Seek and you shall find; Knock and it shall be opened to you.

Stay healthy.

You cannot always lead others to act out your intentions if you are ill. Hill proved it for three days. He was not always available when he was needed. He was ineffectual, and by extension, delinquent in his performance thereby contributing to the defeat of the South. Take care of yourself everyday so that you, your team, group, company or family can perform at its best.

Make your talents known.

If you have Hill's talent and enthusiasm, but you are not appreciated, there is always someone looking for good talent, and it will be your enthusiasm that will influence someone to tap your abilities.

Impulsiveness clouds judgment.

Henry Heth

Because of similar social backgrounds, Heth was the only Confederate officer Lee addressed by first name. He also had something in common with George Pickett: both graduated last in their classes at West Point. Previous accomplishments that were more reflective of attitude than academic performance made it easy for one of his commanders to recommend his promotion: "I consider him a most excellent officer, and gallant soldier...there is no man I had rather see promoted than he."

At Gettysburg he was spoiling for a fight. He wanted his ragtag Confederates to go into the small town with the excuse of confiscating supplies, even as reliable information from a less experienced officer warned him not to commit to such an action. Both he and his superior ignored the warning, and the battle of Gettysburg began. He wrote later that his intent was to "feel the enemy," and when his army was torn to pieces along the way, he concluded with an almost obligatory but laughable understatement, "the enemy had now been felt." It was a sterile admission perhaps meant to anesthetize his wounds of failure, or to cover up his disobedience of Lee's orders not to engage the enemy until the moment was right. It became evident that Heth's moment was wrong.

To deflect from a miscalculation of his competitor's strengths and a rash decision not to employ a cavalry escort or forward detachment, he engaged in two lies by declaring that his encounter was against "overwhelming forces," and that his soldiers "accidentally stumbled into this fight" in pursuit of shoes. Then he manufactured an accusation that he knew would have Lee's agreement: "Had our cavalry been in position, chances are that the battle would never have been fought at Gettysburg." What Heth misjudged in his arrival at Gettysburg was the clear thinking of an outnumbered and stubborn opponent in Union General John Buford ‑ Heth's exact opposite in terms of anticipating and planning.

Later in the battle wearing a new and oversized hat stuffed with paper for a good fit, he was struck in the head by a bullet. He was knocked unconscious for a time and prevented from participating in the rest of the fight. Heth seemed predestined to be at the wrong place at the wrong time.

It was later asserted by a fellow officer that Heth's real intent was to capture some Yankees and present them to General Lee as a trophy, which would be tantamount to a sophomoric demonstration of his new division command abilities. In terms of job performance "Harry" Heth was impulsive and reckless. Years later he was candid enough to suggest that the battle at Gettysburg "was the result purely of an accident, for which I am probably, more than anyone else, accountable."

Gettysburg Lessons

Impulsiveness clouds judgment.

Heth is a fine example of what *not* to do. Before you attempt to ride half-cocked into the sunrise of success, have a map of your future and understand over what roads of life you want to travel. Read the roadside warning signs for scams. Watch for potholes of self-deception. Obey the speed limits of progress. Observe the guardrails of discipline. Attend to the curves of competitors. Stop by the scenic areas of opportunity. Sing of your ride over the hilltops of success. Learn well as you look into the rearview mirror of your mistakes. Most importantly, keep your focus completely on your destination - your goal. Success comes from being led by all sorts of influences.

Emphasize quality.

John Buford

He drove himself so hard that doctors declared him dead from exposure, exhaustion, and typhoid fever at the age of thirty-seven. He had distinguished himself earlier in the war by leading the first cavalry charge for the Union, and was wounded badly enough to keep him out of combat until the next year.

The recent promotion of "boy generals" in the Union army annoyed this seasoned veteran. Just days before the battle, he ordered the hanging of a young spy. When local citizens protested the hanging, he responded with mocking wit: he would not send the spy to Washington on the basis that he might return as a brigadier general.

An after-dinner pipe-smoker, he was a quiet gentleman of small stature; to his men he was "Old Steadfast." He would give them credit without ever accepting it for himself. They learned to trust their leader and would follow him anywhere, even if it meant suffering the exhaustion of riding on horseback for thirty-five miles in one day. As general of a cavalry unit, he had to keep watch for enemy positions, placing lookouts at strategic points to assess strengths and weaknesses. By the time he reached Gettysburg, his horses and men were exhausted, but that did not stop him from sending out scouts to detect enemy locations. Unlike many generals who were fixated by self-promotion, Buford was strictly business.

The devotion of his men gave him reason to make frank observations about dangerous situations. When one of his subordinate officers expressed certainty about holding his own position on the next day, Buford replied with sobering bluntness: "No you won't!...You will have to fight like the devil to hold your own." Like most generals under fire, while he inspired confidence, he was apprehensive and anxious.

Before the first day's fight began, he was staking the ground on which America's greatest battle would be fought. He maneuvered his outnumbered men into positions that would buy time for Union General Reynolds to counterattack with a force larger than his, confuse the enemy, and allow the Union army time to slow down the enemy advance. And he did it all while notifying his commander: "My men and horses are fagged out. I have not been able to get any grain yet....Facilities for shoeing [my horses] are nothing....I can get no forage nor rations; am out of both." Even with limited resources, his casualty rate was less than five percent, one of the lowest in the fighting that day. It was Buford who created the first link in a chain of decisions that would eventually turn the tide in favor of the Union. In his official report he remarked: "A heavy task was before us; we were equal to it, and shall all remember with pride that at Gettysburg we did our country much service."

Gettysburg Lessons

Emphasize quality.

Some would suggest that it is the quantity of resources rather than the quality that makes a difference. Buford proved the opposite. Not having enough can influence you to focus more sharply on what will lead you to your objective. In 1975, Marva Collins of Chicago received national recognition as a "miracle worker" with inner-city black children because she was able to make scholars out of troublesome youths, not with inferior classroom conditions that suggested a genuine lack of money, but with the desire to influence children with a better perspective on their futures. She and Buford were effective because they worked with the *quality* of what they possessed and ignored the *quantity* they lacked.

Be a team player.

By being himself with no desire for fame, Buford understood that he was part of a larger team, the Union army. As a team leader, your unglamorous effort and simple focus can be responsible for influencing your team to win.

Major odds require risks.

John Reynolds

After meeting John Reynolds, Abraham Lincoln called him "our gallant and brave friend." Dashing, energetic and courageous, he was considered one of the most competent leaders in the Union army. One army officer described Reynolds as "a superb looking man...and sat on his horse like a Centaur, tall, straight and graceful, the ideal soldier." Upon seeing Reynolds in the distance, one anxious cavalryman blurted out, "Now we can hold this place."

His sense of fairness gave him an extraordinary reward. A year before Gettysburg, instead of plundering a town he captured, he insisted on his troops' respect for the property rights of its private citizens. When he was captured and became a prisoner in the same town one month later, these same citizens petitioned Confederate authorities for his release. Reynolds became a free man.

Unlike many officers who gained their high rank through political connections, he earned his promotions based on performance. Past duties on the Western frontier earned him the position of Commandant of his alma mater: West Point. But Reynolds refused an offer to be the commander of the Union's largest army because he detested the politics of the highest command echelons. To the individual who took command, General Meade, he wrote a brief message prior to the battle. Never one to bluster he promised to fight the Rebels "inch by inch, and if driven into the town [of Gettysburg] I will barricade the streets and hold him back as long as possible." Meade's response was predictable: "That is just like Reynolds, he will hold out to the bitter end."

On the morning of the first day's battle, he offered a woman five dollars (the modern equivalent is eighty-five dollars) for the breakfast she made for him. When she refused, he told her, "Take it, for I may not live to come back this way and reimburse you for your great kindness."

Once he was on the battlefield he soon discovered that he was up against a numerically superior foe. Several divisions of the Union army had not yet arrived at Gettysburg to gain the right location in the time needed to do battle as one massive body. Reynolds's job was to purchase both time and location. He took a calculated risk and decided to lead an attack that was so vigorous and violent that it would deceive his opponent into thinking they were outmatched. It was psychological warfare at its best.

Reynolds believed that men were better fighters when properly led. "His whole brigade is most decidedly attached to him," said one of his aides earlier in the war, reflecting on Reynolds's relationship with his men, "and I do not think the love of any commander was ever felt more deeply or sincerely than his." Reynolds led admirably, and his men responded by fighting admirably, but the consequences for their beloved leader would quickly turn tragic.

Reynolds succeeded in deceiving the Confederates that their opponent was formidable. After all, they were up against the Union army's famous Iron Brigade, with seasoned fighters whose reputation for "iron" resolve was well known. Still, the Rebels' greater numbers would eventually gain the upper hand. Nevertheless Reynolds's delaying action, at a staggering price in casualties exceeding sixty percent, was able to gain the time needed for the Union army to position itself against the mounting odds of the moment. In leading the attack himself, a move not required of an officer with the rank of general, he was killed instantly with a bullet burrowing into the back of his head.

Gettysburg Lessons

Major odds require risks.

A very strong competitor can influence you to take risks that need to be calculated to gain advantage. Along the way your attitude of fairness with associates will be a big help. By achieving position and time, Reynolds proved that competition is a positive influence in disguise.

Teach by example.

George McFarland

The battle of Gettysburg was won by a dedicated group of teachers. That was the proud claim made by a school principal, George McFarland, who fought there. "The victory at Gettysburg," he wrote, was "the work of the teacher!" McFarland was in charge of some one hundred educators who made up a quarter of what became known as the "Schoolteachers' Regiment." His claim had universal appeal: the attitudes and convictions of the fighting men on both sides were the assumed result of the impact teachers had on their lives, long before they arrived at Gettysburg. "Who that reflects," he concluded, "upon the costly sacrifices the teachers of our country made both in their own persons and in those of their pupils, can doubt this?"

George Fisher McFarland worked on the family farm as a youth and attended school for several weeks during the winter. After doing occasional work on boats that traveled on Pennsylvania's Susquehanna Canal, he began teaching at the unusually young age of sixteen. At age twenty-one he was elected principal of an academy. An educational entrepreneur of sorts, he bought and principled his own academy three years later. When Lincoln called for more volunteers for the war effort in 1862, McFarland closed his school and recruited his own teachers and students to form a regiment of volunteers.

After doing guard duty in Virginia, these volunteers marched toward Gettysburg with a mission. "We are approaching the state of our birth," McFarland explained in a letter to his wife, "not to enjoy peace and comfort there, but to drive out the invading foe. But they will pay for their temerity. They will not long pollute the soil of Pennsylvania with impunity." McFarland could not envision the price he and his men would have to pay for their convictions.

His patriotism was shared with his fellow teachers: "I regret the loss of the many gallant patriots who lost their lives or received honorable scars in its ranks; but I rejoice it was in the battle of Gettysburg and in defense of human freedom and republican institutions."

Like so many other moments in this battle, McFarland found himself in a position of having to purchase one of war's most precious commodities - time. Being outnumbered, bravery alone could not stop the Rebel advance.

Instead of ordering his soldiers to concentrate their fire at an approaching enemy mass, he had them aim and shoot at specific individuals. His fire, he later wrote, had an "effectiveness which the enemy himself respected and afterward acknowledged..." [The enemy] "suffered very heavily from our deliberate...fire..." Confirming McFarland's assessment, a Southern officer later offered the compliment that "the enemy [was] stubbornly resisting."

His observation about the fate of his beloved schoolteachers and students was sobering: "...my gallant officers and men fell thick and fast." Witnessing the carnage, McFarland never imagined that another Confederate officer would honor the schoolteachers' fighting as "the most destructive fire of musketry I have ever been exposed to."

The battered remnants of his regiment had regrouped behind fences and trees to withstand another Rebel onslaught. McFarland was shot in both legs and would lie in his own blood for two days before receiving medical attention. The wait and crude surgical skills caused the amputation of one leg; the other caused him discomfort for the rest of his life. McFarland's commander, General Abner Doubleday, had no doubt as to the sacrifice made by the school teachers on this first day: "...they won, under the brave McFarland, an imperishable fame...and enabled me, by their determined resistance, to withdraw...in comparative safety." With four hundred and sixty-seven men going into the battle, the Schoolteachers Regiment suffered an astounding casualty rate of more than seventy percent in less than seventy-two hours. The enlistment period for McFarland and his men was to expire in less than thirty days.

Gettysburg Lessons

Teach by example.

Billboard leadership occurs when you do what you advise everyone else to do; you are advertising your leadership ability by walking the talk, and the world is truly influenced by it. Parents are the first teachers and leaders. What they do, suggests McFarland, has such a powerful influence on their children's actions and moral framework that it determines the outcome of wars. What you say or do, be it positive or negative, is the origin of someone else's thought or action. Whether you realize it or not, you always have an influence; you are always leading.

Narrow your focus.

As McFarland instructed his men to aim carefully at individual targets, they were more effective in achieving their larger objective. In other words, break down your goal into smaller goals. For example, to lose twenty-five pounds in six months, aim to lose sixteen ounces every week; to read an assigned book of two hundred and eighty pages in two weeks, read only twenty pages a day; to read this book for maximum gain, read only one section at a time.

Teach and lead at any age.

You can be sure that McFarland started teaching earlier than at age sixteen. What he said and did as a child influenced his parents and childhood friends. Young mothers complain about the "terrible twos" because they believe a two-year-old exercises too much influence on the parent who resents having to follow.

Improve yourself with adversity.

James Archer

Archer would disclaim two memorable nicknames: "Sally," for his youthful feminine-like features while a student at Princeton, and "The Little Game Cock," for his bad temper. Before his first battle he was despised by his own men for being cold and tyrannical. But the temper of combat changed him considerably. After his Tennessee men saw how well he performed in a fight and the courtesies he extended to the lowliest soldier, he became a leader they respected and admired. One of his subordinates commented that he had "wonderful judgment and conduct on the field..."

On the first day of the battle, he was somewhat resistant to his commander's order to move forward because he saw that support was too far in the rear. Still confident about his men's ability to thrash the enemy, he forged on but into a surprise enemy advance, which was a virtual ambush. Sick with a fever and physically exhausted, he could not escape fast enough and became the first of three Confederate generals to be captured during the three days. For Archer the war was over.

It was customary for a captured officer to hand over his sword to a capturing officer of equal or higher rank, but on this day his offer was rejected. To add insult to indignity, he was forced to give his sword to an excited private from Wisconsin who simply wanted a trophy. Then Archer came face-to-face with an old acquaintance who was now his adversary. Extending his hand with a smile, the Union commander Abner Doubleday was decidedly amiable: "Archer! I'm glad to see you." Not in a mood characteristic of a festive reunion, Archer snapped, "I'm not glad to see you by a damn sight!" When victory smiles, defeat growls.

Gettysburg Lessons

Improve yourself with adversity.

It was not until Archer was faced with deadly situations that he became "human" to the men who detested him. By enduring the same fears as his own men in combat, he was able to relate to them in ways he had never known. Once his subordinates sensed that he understood them and their needs, they gave everything they had. Now he was influencing his men's behavior in response to his men influencing him with theirs. Archer also proved that you can treat adversity with peers as a personal improvement opportunity.

Keep a sense of humor.

Humor is attitude with latitude, the ability to handle difficult moments with a positive frame of mind. When you look at your situation in a negative light, as Archer did, you will not see the positives. It is worthwhile to associate with people who influence you to be positive and make you laugh. In addition, rent your favorite movie comedy. In short, recharge yourself.

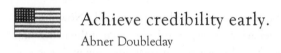

Achieve credibility early.

Abner Doubleday

He fired the first cannon shot of the Civil War from Fort Sumter. He had no more reputation for tactical brilliance than he had credibility as the originator of baseball.

Doubleday was in the fifth inning of the war, but he never made it to second base for recognition of a command performance on the field. He was dependable, but slow to act. His army nickname, "Old Forty-Eight Hours," was an amusing play on his last name. He did not fear leading, but he was reputed for "lacking brains." A negative perception of him was the status he was forced to endure before he took command on the first day. Doubleday was an individual who could render suspicious any action he took. As a result, whatever leadership qualities he demonstrated were never fairly credited at Gettysburg.

Even with this handicap, Doubleday gave an admirable performance with the odds against him. He was successful in taking advantage of a Confederate position and capturing their general. But the tide of the fight turned against him from an enemy of far superior numbers. He did what many commanders would do in the same situation: he ordered a retreat to minimize his losses and to secure a better position from which to continue the battle. Based in part on misinformation that he ordered a premature withdrawal, he was quickly relieved of his command. He became a victim of his own reputation.

Despite the support of his subordinates who considered him a man of courage under very difficult conditions, one whose quick decisions on the first day could have earned him the new moniker of "Speedy," he lost the desire to pursue another battlefield command. The rebuke of his superior left him resentful and bitter. Perhaps he recognized that the perception of him had become a liability he could no longer bear, or overcome, and he simply gave up.

Doubleday was a man of a double irony: he was credited for something he did not invent, and discredited for something he did not do.

46

Gettysburg Lessons

Achieve credibility early.

Doubleday had little credibility with the officer corps before Gettysburg. Achieving small successes early will influence others to recognize your competence, reliability, or trustworthiness. Subsequently, if misunderstandings occur about your actions, you will be in a better position to present arguments to the contrary. The odds will be in your favor to gain support from others, maintain your reputation, and receive fair treatment from those in authority. It could mean your turning a potential foul ball into a home run.

Stand up for yourself.

When you are unfairly categorized or labeled like Doubleday, you have the right and obligation to set the record straight. Saying nothing implies silent agreement. State your case without prejudice and emotion, acknowledging that everyone makes mistakes in judgment. People are generally fair. If you explain yourself, you will influence others to see you in a positive light.

Root out the negative.

Doubleday failed himself by not approaching his accuser. To maintain high morale in any organization, confront privately the person who is making negative ripples. Do not back the person into a corner with no option to save face. Ask open-ended questions and look for answers that dispel negative impressions. Talk it out. If the problem is a person who likes to spread gossip, get rid of the problem. Otherwise, the result is misinformation, misimpressions, and maybe missed opportunities to utilize talent you could have misjudged.

Empathize.

O. O. Howard

Oliver Otis Howard would be a teenager's worst nightmare, always nagging about acting responsibly. His men, mostly German immigrants, grew tone-deaf to his persistent preaching against the evil twins of playing cards and drinking alcohol. Howard's irritating display of religious sentiments and moral superiority added to the resentment his men held against him, which translated into near disasters in battle.

As a soldier who sprang from a military textbook, no one ever doubted his sense of responsibility to command, or questioned his courage in combat. In fact, he lost his right arm in an earlier fight for which he would later be awarded the Medal of Honor.

Referred to by historians as "one-armed Howard," he was obsessed with a need to have an impeccable reputation as a commander. After being in charge of a retreating Union army on the first day, he was relieved of command a few hours later. This was not due to any incompetence since his forces were simply outnumbered, and he was unexpectedly thrown into a command posture without a briefing from the officer he replaced. During the heat of battle and in a fatalistic and overdramatic note to his superior, General Meade, he wrote that the reality of being replaced would be, in effect, the earthquake that would shake his career: it "...has mortified me and will disgrace me. Please inform me frankly if you disapprove of my conduct to-day, that I may know what to do." Moreover, he worked diligently at polishing his image because he could not rely on his own men. He never realized that had he treated them with an attitude of fairness and tolerance, they may have reciprocated and given him the reputation he dearly sought.

Given their hostility towards him and his contempt for their "sinful" ways, he was not perceived as an effective or empathetic leader. One junior officer wrote that "...very little confidence is felt in General Howard. Troops without confidence in their leaders are worth nothing." Perceptions aside, his performance was quite remarkable. Given the overwhelming stress under which he had to operate, he carefully and without panic plotted a fall-back maneuver to a defensive position that

48

proved essential to final victory. Congress later expressed its gratitude for his performance.

After the war Howard's strident advocacy for the freedom of slaves motivated him to co-found a school exclusively for freed slaves, Howard University. In what amounted to one of the Civil War's great ironies, this gesture was empathy of the best kind.

Gettysburg Lessons

Empathize.

If you are going to wear your beliefs on your sleeve, if you are going to tell people how they ought to behave, prepare to be scorned. If you are perceived to have qualities that are admirable in a leader, such as having a little warmth and understanding, you can influence others to help you achieve your goals. Empathy knows and understands what others feel and think. Good leadership decisions do not depend on empathy, but good leaders take into account the expressed thoughts and feelings of others when they are useful to achieve a desired result.

People want to help you succeed.

Had Howard's men respected him, they would have been driven to achieve his objectives. Allowing someone to help you gives that person a sense of personal worth while giving you the results you desire. If you want to observe how successful you can be at leading, ask this powerfully influential question: "Can you help me?" The question achieves two results: first, people are eager to prove a positive trait about themselves; and second, it is an invitation to express their own sense of personal value. This is why a perfect stranger, when you ask for help, will nearly always give you directions when you are lost. One of America's most influential public speakers, Zig Ziegler, is fond of saying, "Help enough people get what they want, and they will help you get what you want."

Intimidation is counterproductive.

When your judgment is challenged, or you do not have the cooperation you seek to achieve your purpose, it could be that others do not understand what you expect, do not see your purpose as achievable, or do not see it as relevant to their responsibilities. To intimidate people to fulfill your wishes is leadership with a negative influence, the kind that handicapped Howard. Lousy leadership is effective because it translates into lousy results.

Work toward the same objective.

If you do not work to influence the confidence of those you lead, expect little or no progress. Followers with no confidence in their leader are ineffective. They are likely to act contrary to a leader's intent. The most progress is made when everyone is working in harmony towards the same objective.

Know your limitations.

Thomas Rowley

A court-martial hearing concluded that he was drunk and disorderly on the first day. Just one day before the battle, Rowley was promoted to lead a greater number of troops for which he had no experience, but he had no time to learn the required skills of managing a larger force. To make matters worse, his men were outnumbered and the confusion of battle only compounded his problems.

As his frustrations mounted, one colonel from Wisconsin noticed him "raving and storming, and giving wild and crazy orders." That was enough to get him arrested and taken from the field. No one but a doctor knew that Rowley was suffering from a case of irritating boils on his thighs, suggesting a direct link between his infirmity and his erratic behavior. Only General Abner Doubleday wanted to credit Rowley for having "displayed great bravery. He was several times struck by spent shot and pieces of shell..." But Rowley's conduct was enough to unnerve a few witnesses on the field.

Given the limitations of inexperience, along with a distracting and painful physical ailment and the blistering heat, it is understandable that the impression he gave reflected a confused man not in command of his senses, that subordinate officers were being ignored, and that his men were not receiving proper orders. Inexplicably, the most troublesome question of all was never asked at his hearing: were men dying needlessly as a direct result of his commanding?

His misinterpreted behavior certainly contributed to a desire by others to see him court-martialed. Due to conflicting testimony at his hearing, his alleged drunkenness was never proven to the satisfaction of Secretary of War, Edwin Stanton, who allowed Rowley to remain in the army.

Gettysburg Lessons

Know your limitations.
Be cautious when accepting a responsibility for which you are not prepared. Find guidance in the form of a study course, seminar, or

on-the-job training. Work with someone who can guide you on how to do things properly. Let someone else influence your progress. Otherwise, you can act with the good intentions of a Rowley, but lack the control you need to discharge unfamiliar tasks. Your actions could also be misinterpreted and your reputation damaged. If you find yourself in such a state, quit while you are behind and seek help. And people will welcome the opportunity to help you.

Failure is a valuable teacher.

Allen Brady

In full retreat he was being chased into town. The enemy was getting closer. It looked like another Union defeat in the making; however, surrender was not an option Brady considered.

Retreating soldiers were usually frantic and disorganized, and if they were fortunate enough to get back to safety, they would be assimilated into other units. When Union soldiers of other units were in total disarray and fleeing, Brady and his men stood in the streets of town exhausted and overexposed to a burning sun. They held off the enemy long enough so Brady could establish an escape route for his men and other Yankee soldiers. He wrote later that the enemy "compelled us to fall back...but not without contesting the ground inch by inch." His intent was to regroup as many retreating men as possible and to establish a new and strong defensive position. The plan worked.

On the next day Brady suffered a shoulder wound by shrapnel, but it did not stop him from leading his men into another fight. Failure was an opportunity to find another way to accomplish his objective.

Gettysburg Lessons

Failure is a valuable teacher.

As a warning sign, failure tells you what *not* to do next. Brady responded correctly. Ultimate failure is not learning, or not having the willingness to learn. It is painless and faster to learn from the failures of others than from your own. That is why we study history, follow a business plan, or listen to role models who have experienced failure and turned it into success. Follow the advice of those who made mistakes, or repeat the same mistakes, experience the same pains, and take longer to get to your goal or destination. Success is yours as long as you recognize the value of failure.

Winners appreciate failure.

Winners and losers both lose, but with a difference: winners have a goal, losers do not. Winners know there is a possibility of losing on their way to a goal, a reality Brady learned quickly. Professional baseball players are inducted into the Hall of Fame because they know they will fail over seventy percent of the time on their way to first base. It is the other thirty percent that earns them immortality. You will never plan to fail, but if you fail to plan you will continue to fail in tests, job performance, and in other challenges in your life. You will blame others for your failure, and you will expect friends, family, and even government to help you. You will be overcome by bitterness because no one wants to help a loser who is not responsible enough to do something positive with his or her life.

On the other hand, it is a self-evident truth that everyone loves a winner. Winners are winners because they plan to achieve. They want to give meaning to their actions and their lives. And they influence everyone around them by their positive behavior. Positive people will only live and work around other positive people. By stark contrast, our prisons are filled with negative people who are surrounded by other like-minded people.

Act upon clear instructions.

Richard Ewell

Despite being the grandson of the first Secretary of the Navy with strong family connections, Richard "Old Bald Head" Ewell grew up in poverty. He later married a wealthy widow and was known for making unusual remarks, such as introducing his new wife by an odd reference to her maiden name, "My wife, Mrs. Brown, sir." His unzipped brand of cursing was well established among most Rebel commanders. Having lost a leg in an earlier battle did not stop Ewell from keeping his command or his spirits.

He performed brilliantly in battle. However, on this day he ordered an attack against General Lee's order not to bring on a general engagement. But Ewell saw a great opportunity to strike the enemy and succeeded. He forced the Yankees to retreat to Cemetery Hill in total disarray. Obliged to change his plans, but seeing a silver-platter opportunity, Lee twice ordered Ewell to follow up his success and attempt the taking of "Cemetery Hill if it were possible" since it would virtually guarantee a Confederate victory. All signs pointed to the possible.

But Ewell did not know if his men could finish what he started unless an attempt was made. In other words, he would know but only if he tried. He hesitated to attack when one of his subordinate generals wanted to push forward immediately, but another general insisted on waiting for support. Ewell's hesitation to act on his own and to obey Lee's repeated order allowed both time and opportunity to slip away. To one angry officer who pressed Ewell to stop ignoring the obvious and attack immediately, he responded in kind, "When I need advice from a junior officer, I generally ask for it." Not taking Cemetery Hill may have been the biggest blunder of the battle. Without the threat of Rebel artillery and Ewell's reluctance to advance, the Union army was gifted with the precious commodity of time to reorganize, dig in, and secure an impregnable position. Ewell did not try, and now all signs pointed to the impossible.

For the moment Ewell was perplexed as to what to do next. He sent out scouts to assess enemy strength only to discover that he was facing an enemy that outnumbered him by at least four to one. He requested reinforcements from Lee, but not enough fresh troops were available. Consequently, he did not attack, but not before Ewell failed again to order another virtually unoccupied hill to be taken when more than six thousand of his anxious men were waiting only a mile away. In spite of impatient junior officers frustrated with Ewell, General Lee, in his usual manner, did not criticize Ewell's decision in his battle report.

Gettysburg Lessons

Act upon clear instructions.

A superior's exact instruction removes all doubt, especially if it is repeated. Communication must be simple and to the point. It is leading by simplicity. If you do not understand an instruction, ask for an explanation. Then repeat what you understand so that there is no misunderstanding. When in doubt, ask; when certain, act. Even with favorable circumstances, Ewell hesitated in the face of an exact and repeated instruction and missed what may have been the opportunity of a lifetime.

Hesitate and lose.

To have no experience in a stressful situation and to try is commendable, but to have experience and not try is inexcusable: you are frustrating your own ability to lead yourself and others out of a bad situation. Ewell was too experienced in his profession not to attempt an advantageous move, but when he decided to do nothing, he lost everything. It is okay to do nothing when you do not have the experience to guide you, but to do nothing contrary to the influence of your own experience will give you the same results it gave Ewell.

Respect those you lead.
Jubal Early

Instead of being their commander, his own men would have preferred him as their target. General Lee referred to him as "my bad old man." Early's discipline was harsh, and his thin-skinned personality would make good on a threat for the smallest infraction. He angered his men with a petition to his own commander to restrict the visits of family members, declaring them, in effect, excess baggage that interferes in the mechanics of war. Though highly combustible and opinionated, his reputation in battle was exemplary, and he was promoted rapidly. Yet it could be argued that he would have achieved more if only he had the devotion of his men. The idea of maintaining morale never crossed his mind.

Early's men, inspired to fight for an independent South, succeeded in spite of him. At Gettysburg they were able and determined to drive the Union army back towards town while inflicting heavy losses. By the end of the first day, his efforts were greatly responsible for Lee's victory. At an evening conference with his generals, Lee asked if Ewell's corps should be withdrawn from a position they fought so hard to gain. In his typically abrasive manner, so he claimed years later, he cut in ahead of his commander Ewell and answered for him. With great irony, Early told Lee that such a withdrawal would hurt morale. His point was well made, that men should not give up a position they had won, but he was missing the point of Lee's game plan for the second day. Lee needed his troops to repeat the day's successful offensive on the following day, which meant being in motion, not still. Not to be insubordinate, Early went on with his duties and never looked back.

Thirty-one years after the battle, Early was self-delusional in his all-too-brief and sterile assessment of the final moments of the Civil War's greatest battle. Pickett's Charge, he concluded, "closed the fighting at the battle of Gettysburg. Meade retained his position on the heights, and our army held the position it had assumed for the attack, while both armies had sustained very heavy losses..." These were fighting words of a half-truth crafting a mythology, but given his demoralized Southern audience, fiction had plenty of readers. The early Early fought to change history, but the later Early labored to revise it.

Gettysburg Lessons

Respect those you lead.

Influence people in a disrespectful manner and you will forfeit your right to lead. Followers want someone to follow, and if you act like Early, you will fail to maximize your achievements. Ultimately, the time will come when you will be forced to change your ways: either lead with a positive influence to get the help you need to succeed, or suffer an assortment of negative consequences.

Expect to be ignored.

When someone else is in control, prepare to have your advice ignored. You may have the most talented supervisor, or you may be the most talented employee, but there is no guarantee that what you suggest at a particular time is going to be taken seriously; Early found out soon enough. No one likes to be proven wrong, but if you are proven correct, a thankful handshake, a warm embrace, or a fast promotion is not always waiting for you. If your advice is ignored, do what Early did: go about your business and channel your energies into the next project or opportunity.

Exercise discipline.
Adelbert Ames

A capable leader and a "boy general" at the age of twenty-seven, he was the first Union soldier in the Civil War to receive the Medal of Honor for his actions at the first battle of Bull Run. His severe discipline in training a group of Maine men earned the same medal for their next commander, Joshua Lawrence Chamberlain, who led them on the second day at Gettysburg. The hard discipline he demanded overshadowed the admiration he earned for his own heroism. Recruits did not give him loyalty, nor did he expect it.

Yet something happened at Gettysburg that could have been predicted. The same Maine men, who once hated Ames for his austere training and seemingly inhuman demands, fought gallantly. They were the first Union force to defeat an undefeated Confederate regiment from Alabama. Ames once considered his trainees despicable, but they exercised his brand of discipline to win. Even though Ames was somewhere else on the battlefield that day, his influence made all the difference on another part.

Chamberlain's men later realized that had it not been for the man they had learned to hate, they would not have survived or received the honorable distinction they earned. After the war, Chamberlain's regiment developed a life-long and affectionate relationship with Ames, the man whose uncompromising demands for discipline not only saved their lives, but was partly responsible for winning the battle on the second day.

Ames was a leader who understood the perils of war, and had the vision for what was needed to prepare men for dangerous risks. He trained them so well that his superiors never complained of high casualty rates under his command. Despite his low profile, his dedication to his own principles of hard discipline exercised the greatest influence.

Gettysburg Lessons

Exercise discipline.

Reflect on the few teachers in your past who gave you too much homework, prodded you to achieve excellence, and made your life seem difficult. Acknowledge that you are a better person today for having learned from them, for having been blessed with their insistent urgings. These tutors taught you not just the rules of survival, but the techniques of excellence. You learned that you have within you the ability to achieve almost anything if you exercise the proper discipline. It allows you to believe in yourself, the most valuable starting point for achievement. The skills learned as a result of the self-discipline you exercise will lead you to wholesome and invigorating successes in your life.

Demand excellence of followers.

To impart the discipline you require of others, communicate the pains they must experience to achieve excellence. Expect no thanks or rewards. They will come in the form of self-satisfaction. Be a mentor, a powerful influence, and enjoy the kind of appreciation that continued for Ames until his death at the age of ninety-three.

Welcome diversity, but...
Carl Schurz

He was ambassador to Spain before returning to the United States to command volunteers from the German immigrant population. But he was a target in a culture of rampant ethnic prejudices. A German citizen by birth and an American soldier by choice, Schurz and his fellow immigrants were scorned as "Flying Dutchmen," an epithet used to suggest innate cowardice of German-born soldiers. Schurz's men did what other troops would have done when hopelessly outnumbered: retreat in a run for their lives. Ridiculed and under the poor leadership of General O.O. Howard in a previous battle, Schurz and his men at Gettysburg, despite an impressive resistance against the opposition, were accused of incompetence and used as scapegoats for much of the Union army's failure on the first day.

Schurz and his men were furious. Behavior was reactionary: they became more defiantly loyal to the language and customs of their old country. With prejudice rearing its ugly head, morale sunk to such a low that Schurz's men had little or no confidence in their own effectiveness as a combat unit.

The perception of his men's poor performance, contrary to what the Rebels concluded, was that Schurz's entire command ran away again in the heat of battle. With history standing by to repeat itself, there was too little time to defend too much ground. Schurz was assigned temporarily by O.O. Howard to lead a much larger body of troops for which he had no experience. He compounded his problem by failing to assume the responsibilities for a larger command and acted as if he were still commanding his old but smaller division. Although thrust upon him in the most stressful circumstance, he was dangerously acting out the Peter Principle: failure was virtually guaranteed by being promoted to a level of competence he did not possess.

In his final report of the battle Schurz wasted no words quantifying the bravery of his men: "Our loss was extremely severe. The Second Brigade...lost all its regimental commanders; several regiments nearly half their number in killed and wounded. Being flanked right and left the situation...was most trying." (Inexplicably, Schurz failed to mention that one of his German-born officers, Captain Francis Irsch, made a gallant stand with six hundred other Union men, and for his efforts was awarded the Medal of Honor.) Accusatory fingers were shaking aggressively that day when unwarranted blame was being assigned to the "foreigners."

Gettysburg Lessons

Welcome diversity, but...

For great things to be accomplished as a group, community, or nation, embrace diversity as a means to an end, a creative force for building unity as a shared goal, something Schurz's superiors never appreciated. Diversity recognizes what each person contributes, and unity channels one's talents toward the good of all. As an end in itself, diversity enlarges our differences, promotes division and hostility, and slowly demolishes the identity of a group. Unity encourages bonding and defines a common identity. It focuses attention and energies on a common purpose and ultimately leads to achievements of all kinds.

Diversity can be a competitive advantage for organizations: people of varying backgrounds and opinions bring unique perspectives to solving problems. Attracting a diversity of talent that is blind to race, gender or beliefs makes a group stronger and its likelihood of success more probable.

Welcome diversity, but only after recognizing that unity is the ultimate force that influences greater productivity and, above all, greater harmony among ourselves. Only then can we invigorate and sustain the meaning of "United" in America's official name.

Human labels are wrong.

Discrimination against race, beliefs, age or gender will damage your efforts to achieve success, be it personally or professionally. Had the unity of purpose not been hampered by discrimination against so-called foreigners, the Union army and Schurz may have been more successful. A label nearly killed Schurz. Consider only positive forms of discrimination. For example, the free enterprise system allows you to choose one service or product in favor of another. Consumers do it everyday. You can influence individuals to deal with you instead of someone else.

Communicate to build trust.

The doors of success open wide to those who make the effort to communicate. The Germans under Schurz proved the opposite by turning communication inside-out, isolating themselves from the world with an emotional self-imposed refusal to communicate. They succeeded in influencing their critics to distrust them. Positive communication, in the form of reaching out, had they tried it, would have proven to be the surest way to influence trust and achieve greater victories.

Consider yourself a victim and fail.

It is possible that a few of these so-called foreigners had already stigmatized themselves as victims of prejudice and decided to exaggerate their nurtured resentment and alienation from the mainstream when everything was finally in their favor. Claiming to be a victim as your identity (versus a problem to be solved), and using it as a self-imposed influence to do nothing, promotes behavior that is unproductive, irresponsible, self-defeating, and perhaps in the case of some of these soldiers, fatal. Whenever the opportunities to win present themselves, however limited, take full advantage or risk failure of your own making.

You can succeed in spite of prejudice.

Wladimir Krzyzanowski

Before the Civil War he was already a veteran freedom-fighter. Born of Polish nobility he participated in an ill-fated Polish insurrection while he was a college student. First cousin to famous composer, Frederic Chopin, he later fled to New York, was penniless but learned to speak English and became a civil engineer in Virginia. At the war's beginning, he raised his own fighting unit in Washington, DC. When its term of service expired, he went to New York to head up what became known as the Polish Legion.

At Gettysburg he had to endure the enemy fire of two armies: the guns of the Confederates and the words of bigotry from American-born Union army soldiers. His men met the same prejudice as Schurz's Germans after the battle of Chancellorsville, a battle that was lost, not because of "foreigners," but because of bad leadership. His unit, made up of Poles, Germans, Czechs, Hungarians, as well as native New Yorkers and Ohio farmers, were determined to succeed in the next battle, to prove their valor and to seek revenge on the enemy.

Hurt by falling from his horse, he refused treatment so he could rally his men from what appeared to be a hopeless engagement on the field. They were outnumbered and were being massacred, but not before they succeeded in driving back one enemy unit from Georgia. One Rebel soldier observed that Krzyzanowski's men "fight harder in their own country than they do in Virginia." But this small victory was momentary. The Rebels came back with overwhelming fire within twenty yards of the Polish Legion. Their commander was able to organize a retreat even though his troops were determined to fight it out to the last man. Confederate General Gordon marveled at the efficiency of Krzyzanowski's movements to the rear.

Krzyzanowski placed his men in a new position, offering temporary relief until enemy cannon fire began decimating what was left of his meager unit. When the bombardment was over, he still had enough men left to support the Union bigots who were engaged in hand-to-hand combat. In an act of selfless glory, he and his men rose above the

64

prejudices of Union men under attack to aid them in their brief but desperate struggle. The addition of his small Polish Legion helped to turn the tide, and a Confederate assault was halted. The Union army was able to hold a position that was crucial to final victory.

Despite heavy losses and the prejudice he had to endure, Krzyzanowski demonstrated that his men were as brave and as American as anyone on the field that day.

After he died in 1887, his body was removed from New York fifty years later for reburial near his old home in Washington, DC. These were some of the remarks made at a special ceremony to honor him:

General Krzyzanowski, whose patriotism we commemorate today, is another link to bind us to the people from which he came in the full tide of youthful promise when shadows lay over the land which gave him birth. It is high privilege to bear witness to the debt which this country owes to men of Polish blood. . . .

These are the thoughts and reflections that come to mind today as we consign to Arlington National Cemetery the honored dust of a son of Poland who faithfully served the country of his adoption. General Krzyzanowski was the embodiment of the Polish ideal of liberty. . . .

These words were spoken in 1937 by Franklin D. Roosevelt, President of the United States.

Gettysburg Lessons

You can succeed in spite of prejudice.
There may be little you can do in the short run to combat discrimination; Krzyzanowski's actions did nothing to lessen the prejudice against his men. Over the long term you can influence others to weaken it. It took a hundred years to go from institutional slavery to the Civil Rights Act of 1964, but most Americans have recognized discrimination as wrong based on ethnicity, gender, skin color and

religion. Americans are growing in acceptance of each other in spite of efforts by those few who want to influence racial and ethnic groups to remain separate.

Never, never, never, give up!

Krzyzanowski never gave up. He was clearly fixed on a goal and nothing was going to keep him down. When your new plan is taking a beating from punches you did not expect, gather what resources you have left and develop a new plan of action. Always keep the door of possibilities open. With no attempt at subtlety Winston Churchill once advised a group of students, "Never, never, never give up!" Not giving up is influencing others not to quit, that success is within your grasp.

Examine your options.

Robert Rodes

Rodes was unlike most other Rebel commanders. He was young, handsome, and described by one historian as "a Norse God in Confederate gray." He was not educated at West Point, but instead graduated from the Virginia Military Institute where eventually he became a math teacher.

Once the war began, he recruited a company of Alabamians and became its commanding officer. He performed so well in one battle that his superior, West Pointer James Longstreet, observed his "coolness, ability, and determination." Another Rebel observer wrote that after he would attend to some detail with his men, he would "ride on again, humming to himself and catching the ends of his long, tawny moustache between his lips." In short, he enjoyed his work.

Rodes suffered injuries in two separate battles, yet his continued bravery earned him a promotion to Major General just before Gettysburg. He became a headstrong commander who took immediate action whenever he saw the opportunity, and his superiors' expectations were growing with each success. But his aggressiveness was going to be used mindlessly as he charged towards his next challenge.

During the battle Rodes went prematurely into an attack posture before learning the strengths and weaknesses of his opponent. Although his charge was successful, it proved too expensive with the loss of some twenty-five hundred men. Instead of taking advantage of an accomplishment, he stopped to reorganize his men when it was more critical to quickly rush and overtake an enemy in chaos. Recognition now came in the form of disapproving comments from associate officers and ordinary privates. He was never again considered a rising star in the officer class, and was never again considered for further promotion. Instead of changing him, the battle marked him.

Gettysburg Lessons

Past performance is no guarantee of future success.

To rely on the successes of past performance, as Rhodes did, can lead to failure, or at least encourage a dangerous complacency that keeps you blind to failure. By their influence your past achievements can influence you to take on new and greater challenges, and give you that extra vigilance to minimize your mistakes.

Examine your options.

The average individual is exposed to thousands of advertisements daily, seeking to influence you to take advantage of "the opportunity of a lifetime." Unlike Rodes, do your homework before acting. Check a proposition for its strengths and weaknesses. Failure to take time to investigate your options can spell disaster.

You cannot delegate total responsibility.
Alfred Iverson

He was unpopular with his troops because of his intransigent command style. More than twenty disgruntled officers under his authority protested his decision to have one of Iverson's friends fill an important position. His response was to have them all arrested. In the next battle he was seen going to the rear for the alleged purpose of finding reinforcements, but the interpretation of his movements was one of cowardice. He had prepared the groundwork for future resentment that simmered for months. It came to a boil at Gettysburg.

He was one of the most emotionally affected commanders on the field during the battle, not to mention the most cowardly. He sent his force into a fight without a twinge of conscience about not leading them, without giving them the direction they needed, or the encouragement they deserved. The full extent of his courage and leadership rested in the last words he gave his men, "Give 'em hell!"

Instead of giving hell, they got hell. Some five hundred of his men were ambushed and massacred within minutes. One survivor from the second rank of formation remarked that he was "sprayed by the brains of the first rank." It was an instantaneous slaughter unprecedented in the war. A bitter private later wrote that Iverson "was drunk, I think, and a coward besides, was off hiding somewhere." Watching from a safe distance, Iverson became entirely unglued at the sight, especially when wounded troops on the ground were waving handkerchiefs or hats in surrender. Iverson's first thought of the massacre was the cruelest judgment of his own men: "I characterized the surrender as disgraceful." But in an astounding turnabout that suggested a face-saving amnesty of his own lack of involvement, without any self-conscious sense of contradiction or hypocrisy, he "exonerated, with one or two disgraceful individual exceptions, the survivors, and claim for the brigade that they nobly fought and died..."

This last phrase was patronizing nonsense. His men were so quickly cut down in this ambush that there was no time to escape the butchery. His bizarre drivel reflected a man clearly out of touch, claiming his men died "without a man running to the rear." Instead of regrouping what was left of his unit and taking blame for what happened, General Alfred Iverson became the Pontius Pilot of Gettysburg, washing his hands of a distasteful responsibility by handing over command to a subordinate officer.

Gettysburg Lessons

You cannot delegate total responsibility.

There can be no short cuts to success, no untested assumptions, no misplaced confidences, no hands-off approaches, no ignoring of possible problems, and no hiding from your responsibilities. You cannot delegate total responsibility. You must assume it all. If you think you can "fake it until you make it," everyone else will rightfully conclude that you will fail. As Iverson demonstrated, negative leadership produces negative results.

Acting irresponsibly and denying ownership of the consequences of your decisions will mean loss of credibility, friends, family, job, and self-respect. Irresponsibility diminishes the self and abandons others to be abused by you.

Show up.

A hands-off approach to leadership is bad leadership. Unless you are fully immersed in your endeavors, you are more likely to make wrong choices, or be too late making the right ones. Become thoroughly involved with the people you are leading, with the problems they are facing, and become acquainted with the solutions you need to reach. Without your involvement, without being available for advice, without constantly communicating your vision of what needs to be accomplished, you cannot expect to be an effective leader and succeed. You cannot expect your business to be successful if your employees cannot contact you. You cannot expect to be successful in teaching if your students cannot question you. You cannot expect to be successful in parenting if your children cannot speak to you. One of leadership's fundamental requirements is being accessible.

Your attitude can save you.

Franz Hubschmann

He grew up in Germany and detested its presumptions of intellectual and ruling class superiority. Once becoming a doctor he made his home in a Wisconsin German community in 1842. After cofounding the state's first German newspaper, he took an active interest in music and became a founding member of a singing quartet, the Milwaukee Males.

Prejudice against foreigners drew him to politics. His tenacious efforts paid off with a one-sentence change he wrote into the state's constitution: "Every person of 21 and over is entitled to vote after one year of residence within the state and his declaration of intention to become a citizen." He was later appointed by President Pierce to be superintendent of Indian Affairs in a four-state area. After his best friend was killed in the Mexican War, he helped his friend's mother by sending her money regularly, a generous act that was not discovered until after his death in 1880. Before the war broke out, he was the acting mayor of Milwaukee.

Principled, educated, and impatient with anyone who opposed him, Hubschmann was captured by the Confederates at Gettysburg and was doing his utmost to attend to the needs of the dying and wounded. Frustrated with inadequate medical supplies, overwhelmed by the number of casualties, working non-stop with no ventilation in near ninety-degree heat, he could no longer tolerate what was going on outside of his church-turned-hospital. With a short fuse on his temper, he dropped what he was doing and marched outside. In a rage, he raised his fist and began to scold Confederate snipers for shooting defenseless Union soldiers who were already wounded. He demanded that they aim their rifles at the healthy ones. The shooting around him stopped, and his captors allowed him to continue treating his overwhelming population of wounded soldiers.

Gettysburg Lessons

Your attitude can save you.

Work with what you have. If you are captured by circumstances in the manner of Hubschmann - feeling trapped by a career or handcuffed by a commitment - look for creative ways to improve your attitude. It will give you a higher altitude to better view the landscape of your possibilities. Lead your supervisor by the influence of a suggestion on how to improve his or her service or product. Many companies reward suggestions with "Employee of the Month" recognition. You may never own a company, but you will never lose the terrific feeling you get from making contributions to an employer's success, not to mention your own. That feeling will release you from drudgery and boredom, and energize you to repeat your best efforts. The world around you awaits your positive influence.

Speak up and get respect.

When you are upset with anyone's behavior, do not be afraid to speak up. Hubschmann spoke up and look what it did for him. You may be amazed with the respect you gain from those who attempt to abuse you. If you do not speak up, the problem does not go away, and it may get worse. Speaking up is aggressive influence that leads others to consider changing their behaviors.

A single act can make a difference.

One can imagine Hubschmann screaming that famous line from the movie, *Network*, "I'm as mad as hell, and I'm not going to take it anymore!" He saved the lives of many soldiers with one screaming protest outside a church. Moreover, he did not accept the prejudice of those American-born citizens who unfairly treated him and other foreigners. He sought to change the system and got a law passed to expand voter rights. He led by the influence of his convictions. As a new citizen, he recognized his right to make or change laws, believed in his ability to make a difference, and influenced enough people to elect him to public office.

Understand the rules.

Horatio Howell

Howell was the only army chaplain killed at Gettysburg. Of all places to die, it was on the front steps of a church; of all reasons, it was for ignoring an elemental rule.

He was born into a prominent Presbyterian family in New Jersey. During his second assignment as pastor in Maryland, he grew to despise the "peculiar institution" of slavery. Under the influence of a mentor, who convinced him that those in favor of disunion were nothing more than a Benedict Arnold and a Judas Escariot, he joined the army in Pennsylvania as a chaplain.

He did not realize that many chaplains were not in favor with the average soldier. Such a sentiment was due to the army's allowing just about anybody to act the role. The War Department soon remedied the situation by requiring all chaplains to be ordained. That did not stop the contempt some soldiers would harbor toward their own chaplains. For example, chaplains had the duty of delivering mail to the troops, but one enterprising minister earned a nickname of "One Cent by God" for charging soldiers a penny for each letter he would deliver to their homes.

Most chaplains performed their duties well in counseling the wounded and dying troops, providing religious services and passing out religious literature. One soldier described the behavior of Reverend Howell: "Our chaplain never failed to administer to the spiritual wants of all who he could interest." Once he reached Gettysburg, he was right in the middle of the fighting in the downtown area. Late in the hot afternoon of July 1, distracted from tending to the wounded in a local church, he went outside to see what was happening. He found himself looking down a Rebel gun barrel.

Instead of raising his hands and shouting the required "I surrender" so that his life would be spared, he began to argue why he was a non-combatant. It did not help his credibility that Howell was uniformed as an infantry officer, complete with ceremonial sword. By one account he raised a hand in a menacing or authoritative manner.

73

With the combination of appearance and gesture, the Rebel aiming the rifle rightly interpreted his adversary, which was a challenger refusing an enemy's order to surrender. In addition to seeing no proof of claims being shouted and no apparent insignia to designate Howell as a chaplain, the Southerner did what he was required to do: shoot the enemy. A rule of war never excluded army chaplains on both sides from being captured, or from being treated as prisoners of war. Howell may have thought of himself as exempt from the rule.

Gettysburg Lessons

Understand the rules.

Before you engage in any activity or competition, understand the rules. Rules lead you to understand your limits, which influence your choices. Abide by them to avoid surprises. Otherwise, like Howell, you put yourself at unnecessary risk.

Avoid winless situations.

Winless situations should be avoided. They accomplish nothing and serve no advantage. There is no dishonor in walking away from overwhelming odds. Hazardous circumstances will nearly always lead you to a correct decision.

Appearances can deceive.

No matter your intentions, you can damage your credibility by doing or saying things that appear unconnected. Howell gave a wrong impression that influenced someone to kill him. Your unsuitable comment or unbefitting gesture can cost you your job, your career, or kill a new relationship.

Age and experience are assets.

John Burns (Gettysburg resident)

He was a veteran of the War of 1812. At age sixty-nine, John Burns was one of the few but oldest civilians to fight in the battle. As a former constable his instincts told him to establish some order in his town. But Mrs. Burns wanted her husband to exercise some common sense in the December of his years, and expressed her apprehensions in no uncertain terms. Patriotic or just plain cantankerous, with an old rifle he left the comfort of his home, the care for his cows, and headed for the nearest fight. His age and past experience prepared him well for this temporary venture. Asked what he did in the fight, he responded: "Oh, I pitched in with them Wisconsin fellers."

At one point in the battle, it was feared that he would be captured and shot on sight as a "bushwhacker." If you were going to fight, you had to play by the rules. One rule said that in order to fight you had to be a real soldier. A quick-thinking officer swore in Burns as a volunteer, a baptism that was followed by plenty of fire.

Burns was wounded three times, and was lucky enough not to have a limb introduced to an unclean hacksaw for amputation. When the Union army had retreated, Burns was detained by a group of Rebels and claimed to be an innocent bystander, careful not to admit to his roll as an enemy combatant. Because the press was hailing him as the "Hero of Gettysburg" four months later, President Lincoln asked John Burns to accompany him to a prayer service on the day he delivered the Gettysburg Address. But Mrs. Burns may have considered her wounded spouse the Shakespearean fool who rushed in where angels fear to tread. To the soldiers with whom he fought that day, Burns was an inspiration, demonstrating that you are never too old to fight for what you believe.

Burns was later eulogized by American poet, Bret Harte:

...John Burns - a practical man -
Shouldered his rifle, unbent his brows,
And then went back to his bees and cows.

Gettysburg Lessons

Age and experience are assets.

Before you become involved in a situation that will demand a great investment of your resources at considerable risk, find a John Burns to influence you on what to do and what to avoid. Look to older retired people, or to those who have lost their jobs, or who are in second, third, and fourth careers. They and many senior citizens possess a wealth of experience, and many are perfectly willing to give it away for the sake of enhancing their sense of self-worth. Mrs. Burns may have been upset that day, but Mr. Burns was feeling the confidence that comes with past experience.

Be competent.

Once you have achieved expertise in a specialty, match your activities with your abilities. Stick with what you know and shine in your competence. It will influence others to judge you fairly as an expert. Otherwise, you stand to be wounded grievously and taken out of an enterprise in which you do not belong.

Enthusiasm is not enough.

Do not take a job as a carpenter if you cannot pound a nail. This is not to suggest that you should not challenge yourself to try something that is foreign to your experience. In fact, try things you have not experienced and obtain guidance on how to master a new skill. If you cannot develop a certain expertise after you have made a reasonable effort, move on to something else. America's most respected basketball player, Michael Jordon, tried to be a baseball player. He quickly learned that baseball was outside of his training and expertise, a sport for which he could not develop a skill, no matter how hard he tried. Predictably, he returned to his area of competence - his area of influence. In the process he got back the confidence he needed to excel on the basketball court.

You are courageous.

Bayard Wilkeson

This nineteen-year-old experienced the unthinkable horror of having to amputate his own leg in an effort to stay alive. It was an excruciating passage into manhood few could ever imagine, let alone endure.

Bayard Wilkeson came from a prominent and politically connected family in western New York. His grandfather's strong antislavery views had a profound and lasting impression upon him. The senior Wilkeson was a founder of the American Colonialization Society that freed slaves, helping them settle in what is today the African country of Liberia.

His father Sam was a reporter for the *New York Times*. Using his influence, Sam secured a commission in the artillery for Bayard, a position he considered less hazardous; however, two years earlier Bayard preferred the front lines of the infantry. Wilkeson took his soldierly duties very seriously, often displaying qualities expected of much older officers: coolness, efficiency and daring.

On July 1, Wilkeson was ordered to take advantage of holding a hill. It would buy time for the Union army to organize its defenses closer to town. Not so calmly, he directed his men to maintain a steady and effective fire. Enemy artillery commanders saw him as a nuisance in the way of a major Confederate advance. A conspicuous target on his white horse, Wilkeson found a dozen cannons pointed directly at his position in a devastating converging fire. An enemy shell went through his horse and mangled Wilkeson's right leg below the knee. With unimaginable courage, he took a small knife from his pocket and cut through the remaining pieces of flesh that kept his leg attached to his body. He ordered four of his men to carry him to a nearby house, and then told them to return to battle.

Wilkeson lay in the cellar of what became a makeshift hospital with wounded from both sides, but with no medical staff. Two women told his father that young Bayard was in great pain and died due to the loss of blood, adding that he was a gentleman through his ordeal. His last act of life was to give his last drink of life-giving water to a wounded but demanding Confederate soldier.

Assigned to report on the battle, Sam Wilkeson was unaware of his son's death until the following day. Over his fresh grave he wrote a father's agonizing question about his son's death that appeared on the front page of the *New York Times* three days after the battle:

> Who can write the history of a battle whose eyes are immovably fastened upon a central figure of transcendently absorbing interest—the dead body of an oldest born, crushed by a shell in a position where a battery should never have been sent, and abandoned to death in a building where surgeons dared not to stay?

Gettysburg Lessons

You are courageous.

If courage is the strength of mind that defeats whatever threatens your purpose, if it is the capacity to endure the worst of circumstances, if it is taking action without regard to failure, then Wilkeson proved that courage is not a virtue restricted to the older and more experienced, but a human quality that reveals itself in stressful circumstances regardless of age.

When challenged by adversity you can achieve what is necessary and lead others to do the same. By your example you are the most motivating influence.

On 9/11 those passengers who quickly rose from their seats to struggle with terrorists on Flight 93 did so in the worst of circumstances, and were influenced by the terrorists and each other to act in a manner that perhaps saved thousands of lives on the ground.

Have fun!

William Smith

As the newly elected Governor-in-absentia of Virginia, he was nicknamed "Extra Billy" for his ability to charge extra for services he performed as manager of a mail service. At age sixty-six, he was the oldest Confederate officer on the field, old enough to be the grandfather of those he led. He spared no verbal expense in his conspicuous contempt for "West P'inters," declaring that common sense was more important than a military education at West Point. Ironically, he was not very competent as a commander. His claim of seeing an enemy presence that never materialized prevented his fellow generals from taking initiatives that could have changed the outcome of the fight. Instead, they waited for an enemy that never came. Smith's lack of common sense, or perhaps poor eyesight, may have prevented the South from winning the battle of Gettysburg. He left the army soon after the battle, and six months later he returned to his office as Governor of Virginia.

An incident before the battle illustrated Smith's approach to difficult circumstances and remarkable timing. Having a flare for public speaking, he could not resist the urge to speak from atop his horse to people in the street whose spirits he thought needed lifting. In enemy territory, addressing mostly women whose men were fighting to ensure that the southern states come back into the Union, he asked, "My friends, how do you like this way of [the South] coming back into the Union?...I have been in favor of it for a long time!... We are behaving ourselves like Christian gentlemen, which we are."

Upon witnessing this spectacle, his commander scolded Extra Billy for causing a traffic jam. True to form Smith responded by saying that he was just "having a little fun, which is good for everybody." It is not known if his humor insulted some of his listeners or inflamed their resentment of the Confederacy. In either case, he led people to a lighter moment in a harmless sideshow of the battle.

Gettysburg Lessons

Have fun!

Smith knew not to take his circumstances too seriously, and to create a light moment when opportunity presented itself. Instead of allowing yourself to be caught up in negative emotions, have a little fun! Humor is what greases the emotional skids of a pressuring situation. It relieves the tension, soothes the pain, and lessens the stress. It is the great equalizer of perspectives.

Recheck your own claims.

When you observe what appears to be a negative situation, double-check your assessment. A misinterpretation will influence you to make a wrong decision. If you do what Smith did, making an observation without checking its veracity, the judgment you make can be disastrous to everyone's interests.

Don't waste your talents.

John Gordon

Although it was highly unusual for combatants, he rarely went into battle without his wife nearby. They were devoted to each other, and she enjoyed his sense of humor except on one occasion. After suffering five bullet wounds in a previous battle, one which scarred his face severely, he wrote: "My face was black and shapeless—so swollen that one eye was entirely hidden and other nearly so...I saw at once that I must reassure her." Hoping to calm her he mused, "Here's your handsome (?) husband; been to an Irish wedding." As if on cue, she let out the equivalent of a new widow's scream. Later she enjoyed referring to her husband's scar as "John's Yankee Dimple."

His vision of an independent South was communicated on the field with such rhetorical eloquence that his men approached him with an extraordinary request. They asked him to refrain from making any more stirring speeches before a battle. One soldier gave this astonishing reason: "Because he makes me feel like I could storm hell." Not surprisingly his unit had the highest casualty rate of any other Rebel unit on the first day. A wounded Rebel remarked: "He's most the prettiest thing you ever did see on a field of fight. It [would] put fight into a whipped chicken just to look at him!" Another recounted that he was "standing in his stirrups, bareheaded, hat in hand, arms extended, and, in a voice like a trumpet, exhorting his men. It was superb, absolutely thrilling." In the saddle he was a monument of inspired oratory.

Gordon succeeded in pushing the enemy back towards town. He wanted to complete the destruction of a beaten foe by following up on his gains. Convinced that complete victory was at hand, his orders were not to engage the enemy further until all of Lee's troops were massed. Gordon would later remark:

No battle of our Civil War—no battle of any war—more forcibly illustrates the truth that officers at a distance from the field cannot, with any wisdom, attempt to control the movements of troops actively engaged.

He was also cautioned by a fellow officer's misinterpretation of a new Union position that would threaten at any time. Gordon waited for an enemy attack that never came. Although tempted to disobey orders because of the certainty of his position, his time and talent were wasted, and for the rest of the battle he did virtually nothing. With the same verbal skills he used to inspire troops before a battle, he could neutralize the impact of an event by downplaying its importance. In his official report of the fight, he offered an extraordinary if not bitter observation of the remaining two days of the battle, "I do not consider of sufficient importance to mention." Frustration came naturally to being sidelined.

After the war, Gordon was asked frequently to speak all over the country about an unusual personal incident he said took place on the battlefield, that he took the time on the ground to fulfill the last wishes of Union General Francis Barlow before he died, only to discover him in a dining room in Washington, D.C. eleven years later. It was a moving and entertaining story as only a great orator like Gordon could tell it. The event about which he spoke so often, for which he received many accolades, and with which he inspired the reuniting of a nation, helped win him the governor's seat of Georgia and a US Senate seat. Today, the Gettysburg National Park Service has an actual glass display that depicts the "Gordon-Barlow Incident."

Gettysburg Lessons

Don't waste your talents.

Superiors do not always use the abilities of their employees. Like the Biblical Samson who had slain thousands with the jawbone of an ass, Robert E. Lee may have done the same with the jawbone of a Gordon. Gordon's rhetorical skills to influence outcomes were not employed in the remaining two days. For a group to excel, the talent of each individual needs to be encouraged frequently. Otherwise, good talent will search elsewhere to find someone who will reward ability.

Verify before acting.

Though Gordon had to wait for further orders to proceed, he received misinformation that came from only one source. Before attempting to influence a superior on a decision, confirm your information more than once. Seek information you can verify to better determine your actions and lessen your risks.

Be part of the action.

Gordon's words remind us of the difficulty of managing any activity when you are not physically present to influence the outcome.

Prejudice damages personal growth.

Francis Barlow

A minister's son and a lousy dresser, he graduated first in his class at Harvard. He went on to become a lawyer and wrote occasionally for the *New York Tribune*. When the war broke out, he left his wife of one day and enlisted as a private. Before long his bravery and commitment were enough to get him noticed by superiors. They eventually promoted him as one of their "boy generals" at the age of twenty-eight. Disliked by his men for being a strict disciplinarian, he wrote, "These Dutch won't fight. Their officers say so and they say so themselves..." Barlow was not immune to the ethnic discrimination that contaminated the country's culture. The so-called "Dutch" were mostly foreign-born Americans who were scapegoats for a Union defeat in a previous battle, even when they did what anyone else would do when overwhelmed by a rushing enemy - turn and run.

The hostility that erupted became mutual. Mistrust by the rank and file was their response to blame from officers. Morale, the emotional glue that holds fighting men together, was totally lacking. For his demoralized fighting group Barlow did nothing. Even the sentiments of native-born troops were best expressed by a Pennsylvania soldier who described Barlow's leadership as "an epoch in our history which will never be forgotten by those who had the misfortune to serve under him."

During the first day of Gettysburg, carefully forming his troops as directed, he led his men to a hill that offered better topography for fighting. Attempting to fill a growing gap in the Union line, the enemy attack grew more aggressive. His men recognized the vulnerability of their position and retreated towards town. It was as if fate had assigned them again to be at the wrong place at the wrong time. Barlow was quick to express his own bigotry against these "foreigners" even though many were clearly American-born. The enemy "had hardly attacked us before my men began to run. No fight at all was made." But Barlow's adversary, Confederate General Gordon, later remarked that Union forces facing him put up "a most obstinate resistance." Barlow's observations about his men were a lie. His tactical error resulted in being so overwhelmed that his attempt to rally his troops was fruitless. In all the confusion of retreat, he was wounded and left for dead.

Alone and in agony from his wounds, another irony of war was making its debut: a group of Rebels carried him back to a home for medical care. A few days later, in a letter to his mother, Barlow unconscionably credited his enemy as "more heroic, more modest and more in earnest than we are." Barlow's words were those of a young man who could not defend his lack of responsibility or his bigotry, which discredited the bravery and resolve of younger Union men who went on to win the battle without him, or in spite of him.

Gettysburg Lessons

Prejudice damages personal growth.

Prejudice was a smokescreen Barlow used to hide his own shortcomings of leadership. Blaming his troops for his own mistakes was signaling a conspicuous lack of character. It is always easier to point the finger at someone else when you fail to influence those who look to you for guidance. Blaming others is Novocain to the soul: you feel neither the guilt nor the need to change a destructive habit.

Compete with facts.

If you have judged your own situation correctly with the help of thorough research, you are in a solid competitive position. Do not let yourself be distracted by what *appears* to be advantageous to you. Barlow did not allow anyone to persuade him to go elsewhere. As a result, he met with disaster. He proved that you can lead yourself toward negative results even when outside forces are influencing you toward a positive outcome.

Focus on results, not excuses.

Barlow used another age-old excuse for avoiding blame for his lack of positive leadership: compliment your competitor. It says the competition has a better product, a better service, a better team, a better plan, a better anything. This excuse keeps the attention away from you and the results you want in the hands of your rivals. Unintentionally, you influence yourself to do the wrong thing, which in many cases can be nothing at all.

You always have an influence.

Barlow's brilliance was wasted. Being smart is not a requirement for leadership. Regardless of how you use your brain, you lead by how you speak and act, and there are consequences - good or bad. In short, Barlow proves that you can be a proven and effective leader when your results are a disaster.

Effort uncovers abilities.

Sarah Broadhead (Gettysburg resident)

She chronicled her pity by what she saw on the faces of captured Rebels in her little town: filth, exhaustion, hunger, fear and hopelessness. Her diary gives us a clear picture of how she responded to the battle. She felt such compassion for one Confederate that she gave him a pair of her husband's boots. It could have been considered a treasonous act to give comfort and aid to the enemy in a time of war, but Americans hardly viewed each other as enemies. This was no ordinary war. It was a fight between brothers and sisters.

By recording what she saw, she was able to give her readers a sense of how ordinary people perform under the most stressful conditions. She was confronted with what appeared to be an impossible task: she was asked to attend to a severely wounded man, which was something she had never done.

I did not know whether I could render any assistance in that way, but I thought I would try...Stooping over him, I asked for his wound, and he pointed to his leg. Such a horrible sight I had never seen and hope never to see again. His leg was all covered with worms.

She helped carry other wounded men from water-soaked cellars of local homes to the fourth floor of the Lutheran Seminary building. Five days after the battle, she concluded: "Some weeks since I would have fainted had I seen as much blood as I have to-day, but I am proof now, only caring to relieve suffering."

Nerve-racking conditions struck her with the force of an epiphany. She learned so much about herself in so short a time that she was able to pen the most persuasive comment about human potential:

...we do not know until tried what we are capable of.

Gettysburg Lessons

Effort uncovers abilities.

Discover unknown talents by doing something new. By contrast, doing nothing new makes you a boring person. You are predictable because you repeat the same activities everyday. By doing something new, Broadhead was influenced by discoveries about herself and uncovered previously unknown abilities. You can do the same right now. Put down this book and do something you have never done before.

Failure is ignoring the obvious.

Jennie Wade (Gettysburg resident)

When the war came to the doorsteps of Gettysburg, most residents had to retreat to their cellars for protection. But there were some who took calculated risks with the exception of Jennie Wade. She has the distinction of being the only civilian killed in the battle. Today there is a statue of her outside the house where she was shot by a sniper's bullet.

Wade and her mother worked as seamstresses to support the family when her father became too ill to work. To earn extra income, Jennie cared for a disabled six-year-old boy. On July 1, along with her mother, brother and the boy in her care, Jennie visited her sister, a woman whose new-born was only five days-old. With bullets flying from every direction, the two boys sought cover. Though frightened, the three women were making no apparent effort to take extra protective measures.

Union soldiers were falling dead and wounded all around them. A 10-pound cannon ball crashed through the roof, but failed to explode. Soldiers who came to the house asking for bread no doubt offered plenty of warnings and advice to seek safer shelter. An additional one-hundred-and-fifty bullets slammed into the sides of the house. Although difficult to imagine, she and her mother acted as if completely unaware that the kitchen in which they stood was between Union and Rebel snipers, an unforgiving, no-exceptions killing zone. To no avail, Jennie's sister finally pleaded with her mother for both of them to take cover.

While ignoring the glaringly obvious explosion of shells and blazing guns outside her door on the morning of July 3, Jennie prepared to make bread. At approximately 8:30 a.m., a single bullet struck Wade from behind, penetrating her heart. Only when it was too late for Jennie did everyone in the house finally seek shelter in the cellar, remaining in relative safety until the next day.

Having willingly placed herself in mortal danger, one could suggest that her statue, one of more than thirteen hundred monuments in the Gettysburg area, is dedicated to either poor judgment or youthful innocence.

Gettysburg Lessons

Failure is ignoring the obvious.

Facts that are inconvenient, particularly dangerous ones, should never be ignored. When a threat to you is real, as it was for Wade, you need to take measures to reduce or eliminate it. Though Wade was a positive influence with her generosity of bread to soldiers, caring for two children, and having a strong religious sense, her apparent naiveté simply frustrated the common sense needed to save her. Wade embodied the values that make America great, but a nation's successful war against a sworn enemy, and ultimately its survival, can make no allowances for Jennie Wade behavior.

Generosity honors you.

Elizabeth Thorn (Gettysburg resident)

She cared for wounded and dying Union soldiers by offering her home as a place to rest and for giving away loaves of freshly-baked bread. Bread was not only a staple, but a symbol of home for soldiers convinced they would never see their families again. Certainly unusual for a woman, Thorn was also the caretaker of the local cemetery while her husband was away fighting for the Union.

In a lengthy account describing her conditions and activities during the battle, Thorn casually mentions: "...I had no bread, for I had given it all away in the morning. But I said I could make cakes..." Her generosity stood in stark contrast to an observation made by a soldier from Maine. He objected bitterly in his diary that "the women [of Gettysburg] have the contemptible meanness to charge us two dollars for a loaf of bread..." (thirty-five dollars a loaf in today's value). Like Esau in the Bible who sold his inheritance for a bowl of soup, it is probable that soldiers were not thinking of the value of money when death was uppermost in their minds. Such profiteering was foreign to Thorn.

She and her sixty-three-year-old father were never fully compensated for digging graves. Nor did she complain about the task, even though her six-month pregnancy was an impediment to a gruesome job that outmatched her stamina. She managed to get help from two of her friends, she wrote, but "...one only stayed two days, then got deathly sick and left. The other stayed five days, then he went away very sick...." Only she and her father buried more than one hundred soldiers, as many as thirteen in one day.

Thorn was remarkable for her selflessness. She made no demands of the government for the loss of personal property, sought no financial gain from the soldiers for baking bread, expected no special rewards for her mortuary services, and did not ask for sympathy for having to care for her three small sons at the same time. For the relatives of those dying men in her care, she was a blessing. The respect she showed for their deceased husbands, fathers and sons undoubtedly provided loved ones consolation and a sense of finality they did not expect from a total stranger.

Gettysburg Lessons

Generosity honors you.

Elizabeth Thorn's actions endure as a reminder of the greatness of our human nature. Thorn demonstrated that within each of us is the capacity for great selflessness that can lead others to similar action. In their generosity, millions of Americans became Elizabeth Thorns following the events of 9/11 and Hurricane Katrina in 2005.

Greed diminishes you.

The soldier's complaint about the cost of bread charged by some Gettysburg women reflects the dark side of our nature. "Profit" is by no means a dirty word, but reaping profits from the misfortune of others, or from your own misery, is inexcusable, as was demonstrated by many victims' families of both the World Trade Center attacks and the Oklahoma City bombing.

Success comes in small steps.
Elmina Spencer

Elmina Spencer was respected for her work with the sick in her local village of Oswego, New York. When her husband volunteered for military duty, she went with him. She spent two weeks on horseback just to reach Gettysburg, which meant hauling some three hundred and fifty pounds of supplies. When the weather was too warm for the soldiers to wear their wool coats, Spencer would volunteer her horse to carry the coats and march beside her husband.

During the first day's battle Spencer found herself caring for the wounded and simultaneously creating a makeshift hospital in a small church located south of the fighting. Among the six hundred wounded she was attending was a young soldier who was shot through the mouth and throat. The surgeons, who had more injured than they could possibly handle, quickly assessed him as terminal since he could not swallow. Refusing to give up, Spencer continually bathed his wound in cold water so that it might heal. She directed the wounded soldier not to ask for any food for a week. Heroically he endured, and miraculously the inflammation began to subside. She was able to close the wound, and at her direction he readily consumed a healthy broth. His health improved and his life was saved.

Another nurse testified to Spencer's endurance and courage: "...the noble woman seemed unwearied in her extensive work or mercy...She often went to...distribute supplies of tobacco whilst the bullets of the enemy were dropping around her."

Gettysburg Lessons

Success comes in small steps.

Add new experiences to your life. Each fresh experience is an influence that leads you to have a little more self-confidence. If you want to write a letter, first learn how to write a sentence. If you want to build a house, learn how to use a saw. Break down what appears to be a difficult job into small, manageable tasks so that reaching a goal becomes a whole lot easier.

Experience guides you to solutions.

When you have a problem, the solution may be in the inventory of your experiences. Let them be your influences. Accept the value of experience and the time to gain it. It leads you to trust your instincts, your intuition, or your "gut." It saved the life of a young man from Oswego.

July 2

The Second Day

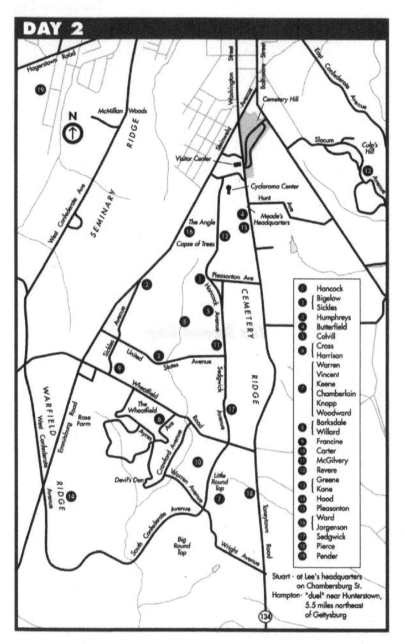

DAY 2

Hogerstown Road

19

N

McMillan Woods

SEMINARY RIDGE

West Confederate Ave

West Confederate Ave

Washington Street

Baltimore Street

East Confederate Avenue

Cemetery Hill

Steinwehr Ave

Visitor Center

Cyclorama Center

Hunt

Ave

Slocum

Culp's Hill

Avenue

13

Meade's Headquarters

4

16 The Angle

13

Copse of Trees

12

Pleasonton Ave

1

Hancock Avenue

5

8

CEMETERY RIDGE

11

Sickles Avenue

United

2

States Avenue

9

Wheatfield

Sedgwick Avenue

WARFIELD RIDGE

West Confederate

Emmitsburg Road

Rose Farm

The Wheatfield

6

Ayres Ave

Crawford Avenue

17

10

Devil's Den

Warren Avenue

Little Round Top

7

18

Taneytown Road

14

South Confederate Avenue

Big Round Top

Wright Avenue

1	Hancock
2	Bigelow / Sickles
3	Humphreys
4	Butterfield
5	Colvill
6	Cross / Harrison
7	Warren / Vincent / Keene / Chamberlain / Knapp / Woodward
8	Barksdale / Willard
9	Francine
10	Carter
11	McGilvery
12	Revere
13	Greene / Kane
14	Hood
15	Pleasonton
16	Ward / Jorgenson
17	Sedgwick
18	Pierce
19	Pender

Stuart - at Lee's headquarters
on Chambersburg St.
Hampton- "duel" near Hunterstown,
5.5 miles northeast
of Gettysburg

134

Be totally involved.
Winfield Scott Hancock

Charismatic at age thirty-nine, his nickname was "Hancock the Superb." He was as superb at directing army divisions as he was at keeping his linen clean. Never one to mince words, he maintained his unbuckled style of profanity in optimal form. Highly regarded by his men, Hancock was able to bring order out of chaos to the point of arresting officers who failed in their responsibilities. A soldier remarked on the "inspiration of his commanding, controlling presence...the fresh courage he imparted...." One of his generals observed that "his mere presence was a reinforcement, and everybody on the field felt stronger for his being there."

He could have been nicknamed, "Win-on-the-Field," for his front-and-center and take-charge approach. To prevail he knew there was a price to pay. His Second Corps of the Army of the Potomac sustained more casualties than any other fighting unit in the federal army. But it also won more battles than any other because he knew there had to be quick group responses to the rapid changes in combat tactics. When asked why he ordered a charge against an opponent when the odds were so overwhelmingly against him on the second day, his own words describe his conviction under great stress: "...it caused me pain to give the order for them to advance, but I would have done it if I had known every man would be killed. It was a sacrifice that must be made." His commitment was unwavering.

Hancock wasted no time. With his dashing to-the-rescue behavior, he raced to the front on horseback, conducted a constant ride-by poll of his commanders, and encouraged them to hold their ground. Warned that he should not endanger his life, his response suggested he was positioning himself for posterity: "There's a time when a corps commander's life does not count."

Victory appeared as history's reward for his commitment; however, it came at the cost of not using the artillery more effectively. He believed that only the infantry could win battles, and that the artillery's real purpose was to maintain the infantryman's morale. For Hancock military ideology was in; integration of military assets was out.

After being severely wounded, he refused to leave the field until the battle was going favorably. He remarked later, "Not a rebel was in sight upright when I left." Soldiers were in awe of his bravery. The determination he instilled in his men on that day appears to have contributed to making Pickett's Charge a major defeat for the South.

His reputation was summarized (or romanticized) by a Union soldier: "I met General Hancock once, and I think I grew a foot and a half."

Gettysburg Lessons

Be totally involved.

Set everything in motion to achieve a goal. Like Hancock, get involved totally in what you want to accomplish. Talk to anyone who can help you. Encourage them in every way to generate the results you desire. Be determined to see your project through to the end. Be willing to adapt to rapid change. Look at each obstacle as a test you must pass, an opportunity in disguise.

Moral values inspire trust.

Hancock had the trust of the ordinary soldier. His credibility and effectiveness were established by maintaining his visibility and constant communication. Every year Fortune magazine publishes its "100 Best Companies to Work For." It usually finds more than fifty publicly-traded companies which operate in the same manner as Hancock, and have an average annual return to shareholders of five percentage points higher than the gains of three thousand other companies. The positive work environments they provide establish trust. In other words, there is a measurable relationship between values and a solid bottom line.

Be judgmental.

Hancock never hesitated to punish someone for doing something wrong. Clarifying and enforcing the difference between right and wrong is the moral code by which families, organizations and nations survive. Clarification demands that you be judgmental, that you make blunt, honest and unapologetic decisions that are grounded in the moral code. Like a bull in the china shop of political correctness, Hancock never considered the hurt feelings of the guilty, nor did he give a sympathetic ear to whiners. Parents become effective when they are judgmental with their children; they are leading with a moral influence. As the arbiter of right and wrong, the American judicial system is built on being judgmental. Act with the same moral clarity and ignore the cultural noise to do otherwise.

Take advantage of other resources.

One of Hancock's few mistakes was not taking full advantage of an additional resource. He could have used the artillery more effectively, but he was satisfied that his infantry could carry the day. It was an isolated but classic case of wearing blinders, thinking inside the box, a kind of reverse leadership that did not allow relevant factors to influence his decision-making. He could have gone outside his expertise as an infantry officer for a joint venture with the artillery to create a more destructive result for the Union army. Instead, he treated the artillery as a morale booster rather than an additional tool to achieve greater outcomes.

Put purpose before ego.
Dan Sickles

He was a genuine cartoon, nearly always illustrating bad behavior. With an aptitude for perversity, he was a thirty-two-year-old man when he married a sixteen-year-old girl. Before and after his marriage, he associated with prostitutes and escorted one into the legislative chambers after being elected to the New York State Assembly. Despite being a schemer and a womanizer, he was elected to Congress nine years later. Before he died in 1914, he was removed from the commission set up to raise funds for monuments to his own men at Gettysburg, due to strong suspicions he embezzled the funds. His family would have nothing to do with him because he was "irresponsible and cantankerous." With a reputation clearly up for grabs, historians enjoy saying that he never grew up.

Sickles was a sinkhole of ethics. With moral relativism as his behavioral yardstick, he never measured his conduct against the norms of anyone shouldering similar responsibilities. A political observer in Sickles' home state once referred to him as "one of the bigger bubbles [of] scum...swollen and windy, and puffed out with fetid gas." Another added, "One might as well try to spoil a rotten egg as to damage Dan's character."

An egomaniacal and thoroughly irreverent Sickles acted with total disregard of consequences. This included shooting his wife's lover in broad daylight in front of the White House. He was the first American to use the temporary insanity defense, which may explain Sickles's ability to rationalize future behavior in any situation. After all, he got away with murder. With pure luck the war came along just in time to distract his critics from attacking his reputation as a murdering, cheating and lying rogue.

Sickles was able to obtain his military position and rank of brigadier general by raising his own brigade of infantry. But as a soldier he was a rank amateur; as a commanding general, not unlike many officers in both armies, he was dangerously inept. The Peter Principle states that people are promoted to their level of incompetence, and

100

Sickles portrayed the definition flawlessly. Preferring to trust his own judgment, his men would see how the definition would play out.

With an inherently oppositional temperament, it seemed almost obligatory for him to change his field position, leaving a hole in the Union line, contrary to the expressed intentions of his commander, General Meade. As Meade's most obnoxious liability, Sickles put battle plans at risk and placed the entire Union army in jeopardy. At a great cost in casualties, his men succeeded in slowing down a strong Rebel attack, but not before another Union general blurted out for the second time: "Keep watching, you'll soon see them tumbling back." Purely by accident, or by taking uncalculated risks, Sickles managed to buy valuable time for Meade who was forced to order the immediate occupation of more formidable positions. It soon became apparent that Sickles's only friend was Lady Luck.

Because of his carelessness, he not only had his right leg amputated from a shell blast that afternoon, but the death toll on July 2 was the highest of the three days. One historian observed that Sickles's actions on that day constituted "the most spectacularly successful failure of the century."

Cynics may be tempted to conclude that he dangerously matched a US Army recruitment slogan, "An Army of One." And if history is the border guard between fact and fiction, it allowed Sickles to smuggle in one last truth-be-damned claim: "I won the great and decisive battle of Gettysburg."

Gettysburg Lessons

Put purpose before ego.
To be a good leader you must influence others to act in a positive manner. Unlike Sickles, purpose must be ahead of ego, team ahead of self, and mission ahead of credit.

Do not tamper with a superior's plan.
Do not change a superior's plan without permission. By its very nature, a plan is a diagram of influence designed to lead in a specific

direction. Only by chance did Sickles's decisions work to Meade's advantage, but at a great cost in human lives.

Be aware of the Peter Principle.

On-the-job experience can make you more effective. However, your superiors may consider your past achievements as qualification enough for a better position. You could be promoted to a level of incompetence where your competencies do not match your new responsibilities. Such was the Peter Principle and Dan Sickles. A promotion can be counterproductive when new responsibilities do not allow time for proper training.

Playing by the rules includes taking risks.

Sickles's contempt for rules put an entire army at unnecessary risk. Rules are meant to be reliable and non-negotiable guide posts. Taking calculated risks is one of the rules of success. Risking failure implies a high degree of confidence, a well thought-out plan, and a burning desire to achieve. Not taking risks is not trying, and not trying is never succeeding. By working with risks you can handle, you will increase your chances of success.

Be an example.

Andrew Humphreys

He loved the military so much that he assigned God to the status of warrior: he considered a soldier's life a "godlike occupation." Never one to hold back his opinions, he once remarked with some wit that war was "a damn fine thing!" but "a very bad thing in the sequel..." He was not one to take himself too seriously, including his troops whose nickname for him was, "Old Goggle Eyes," for the glasses he wore. In blunt self-deprecating terms he described a brilliant field movement of his men at Gettysburg: "...it was prettily done....a beautiful sight...resulted in nothing."

Before the war he established his engineering reputation with a book, *Report on the Physics and Hydraulics of the Mississippi River*. His desire for combat easily replaced his engineering tasks when war broke out. Besides having a flare for eloquent profanities, he was highly skilled and possessed a never-give-up determination. He gave personal attention to every detail of a task, and fully exposed himself to danger when he thought it would motivate his troops. Before a previous battle, he stated cavalierly to his junior officers, "Young gentlemen, I intend to lead this assault. I presume of course you will wish to ride with me?" His actions positively shaped the attitudes of his men and won their admiration. His example empowered them to do things they would not think of doing otherwise, such as putting their lives at extreme risk. With luck strikingly similar to that of the Continental Army's George Washington who was never wounded in battle, Humphreys was the Union's Untouchable.

He never received a medal for bravery (medals were intended for enlisted men), but he was the one general officer who could have earned many promotions for his conspicuous gallantry whenever he fought. On July 2, he was ordered to move his division forward in what turned out to be an untenable position. His reserve unit was ordered to move away to reinforce another Union commander in similar trouble, forcing an infuriated Humphreys to declare the movement as "disgusting." Once the Confederate attack was directly in his front, Humphreys was forced to retreat. Again at great risk he gave personal attention to every movement of his men. At one point his horse was shot from under him. Without a moment's hesitation, he grabbed another horse nearby, mounted it and continued to rally his men to the safety of a nearby ridge. Nearly fifteen hundred casualties had to be left behind. Many of his men were not fond of him before the battle, but one soldier remarked years later that they liked him afterward. For his bravery he was awarded a promotion to major general immediately following the battle and was given an offer to be the chief of staff to the commanding general. True to character, Humphreys considered the offer "hell" since he relished the intensity of combat.

Gettysburg Lessons

Be an example.

Be an example to influence and empower others. You will be seen as having values to do the right thing and the skills to do it. A group will nearly always reflect the person in charge. By definition, examples lead.

Demonstrate commitment.

If you expect others to "go to the mat" for you, be willing to do the same for them. The Humphreys difference is this: you must go first. You must demonstrate your pledge to something before you demand that others to do the same. To influence, follow first, that is, follow an idea, and commit to a goal and a plan of action. You will be influenced to succeed, and you will lead others to see the wisdom of your ways. The commitment of those around you may not be as total as yours, but in the long run you stand to inspire enough dedication to help you get what you want.

Negative attitudes fail.

David Birney

He could have been the smart school kid who convinced himself he did not need to study. He even cheated when it suited him. When he was caught, he put the blame on someone else, or begrudgingly admitted his wrong later. General David Birney demonstrated such childlike behavior on the second day.

He annoyed junior commanders from other units for ordering their troops to support his own; he did not have the authority, nor did he seek permission. Was he pulling rank? Very likely. Was he in danger? Definitely. In the messy details of combat, confusion set in with no clear authority or direction. Troops did not know where to go or whose orders to obey. It was a desperate situation where a desperate commander was making dangerous decisions. It is difficult to imagine what choices he had, but clearly he was in over his head. His decisions contributed greatly to the destruction of his own forces, prompting him hours later to remark awkwardly, if not pathetically, "I wish I were already dead."

Commenting on the day's events, General Humphreys criticized Birney severely: "Had my Division been left intact, I should have driven the enemy back, but this ruinous habit...of putting troops in position & then drawing off its reserves & second line to help others...is disgusting."

That evening, in a meeting with all the senior Union commanders to discuss the future of the battle, a self-loathing Birney was the only field commander who suggested that the Union army could not win. Perhaps he assumed that his comrades' command abilities were equal to his. Like a defeated schoolboy, if he could not pull it off, no one could.

Gettysburg Lessons

Negative attitudes fail.

By not accepting the harmful results of his actions, Birney found it easy to suggest that no one else could have done better. This kind of juvenile thinking leaves no room for flexibility that can result in better decisions. Not admitting your mistakes is prescriptive for making new ones. The greatest mistake is a negative attitude. It is expressed in these all-too-familiar statements, "I can't," "It's too hard," "The other team has the best record," "I'm too short," "I'm not smart enough," "I'm black," "I'm white," "I'm too old," "I'm too young," "I'm overqualified." You can change these attitudes by forming clear, concise, and realizable goals that have the energizing influence to achieve them.

Be credible.

Daniel Butterfield

Every time you view a military funeral, or attend a Memorial Day salute to America's war dead, you will hear the musical notes he ordered a young private to write: *Taps*, originally known as *Butterfield's Lullaby*.

A scholar and former law student, he earned the Congressional Medal of Honor for picking up a fallen flag and bravely leading a charge in a battle one year earlier. By contrast at Gettysburg he did sloppy staff work for the commanding general of the Union forces, George Meade. Disliked by other generals who had to report to his boss, one of them remarked with prophetic accuracy, "...that he knew Butterfield well, that he was a bad man & feared Gen'l Meade would regret retaining him." When orders were given to shift a large body of soldiers from one position to another on July 2, he failed to send orderlies or staff officers to guide them. That left twenty-five hundred men in suspension when they could have been used to defend important positions.

His apparent incompetence took a seemingly positive turn. To his credit Butterfield had taken it upon himself to draw up a contingency plan of retreat in case Meade found his forces in serious trouble, a plan that would anticipate nearly everything the enemy might do. It was Meade's method of operations to anticipate every contingency, but since he did not order any retreat plan, it is entirely possible that Butterfield was only anticipating his superior's wishes.

What Butterfield did not anticipate was the bitterness he would cause by not telling his commander about it, and later proclaiming that Meade had actually intended a retreat. Butterfield professed later to be following orders from his superior, but Meade made no such request and only learned of Butterfield's plans of retreat eight months later. It was a startling piece of revisionist history in the making. For sinister reasons Butterfield's version of the retreat story was intended to benefit his friend and Meade's most contemptible critic, Dan Sickles.

Butterfield lied repeatedly to certify unfounded claims by Sickles. The controversy he unleashed was not settled until thirty-five years later when Alexander Webb, one of Meade's generals and now his one-man truth squad, weighed in with convincing statements regarding the absurdity of the retreat allegation. Webb's return fire scored a direct hit, and Butterfield's years of harvesting a dual crop of controversy and ill-feeling came to an abrupt end. Instead of passing into history with military distinction, he stewed in the toxic juices of his own making and slithered into obscurity.

Gettysburg Lessons

Be credible.

Butterfield proved his bravery in battle, but he forfeited his honor by confirming his duplicity. If people come to know you as a fraud, you will influence them to distrust you. Isolation from others will be your fate.

Get along with cohorts.

In the world of office politics where one person may engage in self-important activities, it often takes the form of disparaging someone else's performance. In a highly competitive marketplace, or in any place, there is no justification for Butterfield behavior. Consistent twisting of the truth will shorten your employment and contaminate any attempts to establish or maintain long-term relationships.

Be honest.

Alfred Pleasonton

As a thirty-nine-year-old general who enjoyed quoting Shakespeare in letters to his friends, he was one of the most self-promoting and loathsome officers in the Union army. He proved that to win a promotion the pen was mightier than the deed. Instead of fighting gallantly for advancement, Pleasonton found it easier to achieve it in writing. As an opportunist in a quest for immortality, he wrote credible, self-serving but misleading reports of his own command performance on the battlefield. In other words, he lied his way to the top.

Along with his commanding officer who was frustrated with nearly every action report received from Pleasonton, his men were aware of his well-practiced duplicitous behavior. One officer wrote that "Pleasanton's own reputation, and Pleasonton's late promotions are bolstered up by systematic lying." With an occasional success, he was taken seriously enough by his commanding officer, whose patience and tenure were about to terminate, that he received the highest cavalry command in the Union army.

One of the functions of the cavalry was to gather information about enemy strength and positions. In addition to being insubordinate to his commander who demanded more reliable information, Pleasanton preferred the word of captured enemy soldiers and deserters. His method of verification was mind-boggling: trust, and don't verify. When he failed to exploit any advantage he would blame someone else, take time off to relax, or use the default claim of being outnumbered. In his mind he was better served by fiction than fact, but it never occurred to Pleasonton that posterity was watching.

Pleasonton's bigotry against foreign-born soldiers would take a shocking twist. He ordered a French colonel to scout a valley with three hundred cavalrymen where it was known that nearly six thousand Confederate horsemen were operating. He was attempting murder by proxy. The officer's valor allowed him to survive, but not before Pleasonton falsely reported that his subordinate was "allowing himself to be surrounded." Pleasonton's character was about to catch up with him.

The intelligence gathering he did at Gettysburg was more the work of a new superior who, upon learning of his reputation, chose not to trust him. Instead of leading cavalrymen into battle, he was reduced to a clerk issuing dispatches. Pleasonton killed his chances for fame with lethal doses of deceit that earned him history's harshest judgment - oblivion. A Shakespearean curtain-closure from Macbeth aptly defines Pleasonton: "...a walking shadow, a poor player, that struts and frets his hour upon the stage, and then is heard no more."

Gettysburg Lessons

Be honest.

Pleasonton's destructive habit of lying is a culturally-allowed standard of behavior. Witness the TV appearances of the straight-faced attorneys who defend their guilty clients, or the political pundits who express a seemingly mindless support for their favorite candidate. You can rise above the norm by acting honestly, which influences others to trust you. Only you and those you influence can experience positive change when you continue to govern your behavior by what you ought to do. By contrast, the influence you have by the dishonesty you demonstrate leads others to ignore you.

The whole truth is not required.

Dorsey Pender

Duty was everything. To his wife he put it in writing: "If I can go see you without any neglect of duty, I will." Yet he was a twenty-nine-year-old general in a personal conflict with his loyalty to the South. After reading *Uncle Tom's Cabin*, he found himself in agreement with the anti-slavery views of the Northern author. He rationalized his new allegiance by focusing on what he termed the "barbarity" of the Union army, believing that "a just God will punish them." Northern was his mind, but Southern was his heart.

A deeply religious man with no appetite for war, his command approach soon gained him a reputation for fairness. "My men say I am hard on them," he wrote, "but that I treat them all alike. It would worry me very much if I had a reputation for injustice."

There was another conflict. He appeared to be in what is popularly termed a mid-life crisis. In letters to his wife, he would often mention how other women would notice him and admitted to a flirtation. She recoiled with a verbal barrage to such expressions of vanity, setting off salvos that bordered on their own private war. Eventually they would see each other and resolve any misinterpretations of their written exchanges.

Given other back-and-forth thoughts about their children and his religious ideas, he may have distracted her from the unpleasant thoughts of his death in time of war. Such willful omissions are common practice of soldiers who are sensitive to the anxious feelings of loved ones.

Robert E. Lee had such a high regard for Pender that he remarked on the second day, "I shall ever believe if General Pender had remained on his horse half an hour longer we would have carried the enemy's position." In other words, for a moment in time Pender held the keys to total victory at Gettysburg. But fate would impose on the Penders. After being wounded, he had his left leg amputated. Due to the primitiveness of surgery, he died a few days later. "What is the loss of a

111

man's life," he once asked, "compared to the good of the country?" When Mrs. Pender received the news of her husband's death, she was six-months pregnant with their third son.

Gettysburg Lessons

The whole truth is not required.

Shielding someone you love from the realities of a bad situation makes good sense. The simple knowledge of hurtful information - a negative influence - can cause undue stress. Communicate only what the other person needs to know when it is in your power to resolve a problem yourself. Guard the hearts of those you love.

Be discreet.

Vanity creates misunderstandings and fuels conflict. To make light of your self-indulgences, as Pender did, does more harm than good. Needless time and valuable energy are spent attempting to correct your influential behavior. You lead individuals to feel uncomfortable around you, and nerves are frayed. To keep some sense of stability in your relationships, work at being discreet so as not to offend.

You can make the right choices.

Pender's personal struggles were troubling. Yours could be the desire to make more money instead of spending more time with your family, engaging in distracting activities that place excellent school grades at unnecessary risk, or adopting an ideology that endangers the security of your own country. You are creating your own spiritual battlefield, which appears as an affirmative action plan for the soul: you struggle to make sure there is no loser. In the quest for balance, you struggle with imbalance. You have not set priorities for what you value most. In the extreme, life has no meaning. Resolve your conflicts by making right choices, ones that will influence your life's direction. The right ones come from working on meaningful objectives.

Sacrifice rewards you.

William Colvill III

He was released from arrest just before he led a charge that became one of the most heroic in American history. At six-feet-five he stood out as a lawyer, a newspaperman, and a soldier. He earned the affection of his men for his irreverence for military regulations that stood in the way of taking care of his men. As a result, he was arrested twice.

A powder keg of fear was about to explode. A gap was opening that threatened the entire Union front. Colonel Colvill and some two hundred and sixty other Minnesotans were the only troops between the oncoming Rebels from Alabama and the formidable Union batteries that were not far away. The commander of the Union left, Winfield Scott Hancock, observed that additional troops would be required to head off the Rebels, but time was too short. He quickly figured that all he needed was five minutes. Desperately looking for troops, he found Colvill and yelled: "My God! Are these all the men we have here?" Without hesitation he simply pointed to the oncoming and screaming Rebels and shouted, "Advance colonel, and take those colors!"

Instantly Colvill assumed that he was being ordered to sacrifice his life and those of his entire unit for the sake of a five-minute gain. As if requesting their consent, he turned to his men and shouted, "Will you go along?" After a resounding affirmative response he yelled, "Forward! Double-quick!"

How does a human being determine that he is going to lead other human beings into a situation where it is assumed that no one will come out alive? How is that decision justified when it is reached so quickly and with total assent from those who are asked?

After being ordered to charge toward an opponent who outnumbered him by at least three to one, Colvill quickly calculated what action was necessary. The speed of that decision was likely based on a composition of moral dichotomies that allowed the ideal to triumph in the most desperate moment: union above secession, equality above slavery, the future above the immediate, and a nation above himself.

113

Murderous fire was coming at his men from three directions, causing Colvill to observe later that "the destruction was awful." He was wounded in the shoulder and foot. The time Hancock needed to close the line was gained at tremendous cost, but he gained more than double his money - at least 10 minutes. The gap was closed and the Union line reinforced.

Colville's Minnesota regiment sustained one of the greatest losses in a single battle: roughly eighty percent became casualties in a matter of minutes, all for the trading of human lives for the clock. To measure the audacity of the charge, the Confederate commander testified that "my men were withdrawn to prevent their entire destruction or capture." Hancock was equally awed: "No soldiers, on any field, in this, or any other century, ever displayed grander heroism."

The sacrifice of Colvill and his men, decided upon instantly, aided in securing the fate of a nation in fifteen horrifying minutes.

Gettysburg Lessons

Sacrifice rewards you.

Colvill illustrates why sacrifice is so vital to our daily lives, that in giving up something you gain something. You can give up watching a movie tonight in order to complete a needed report for delivery tomorrow; you can give up a party with friends tonight in order to meet with one of your children's teachers. Repetitive sacrifice creates a habit that influences positive results. Progress on important and difficult issues rarely occurs without some level of sacrifice. To get something in return, determine what you are willing to give up. The more effort you make, the more results you get. Or, the harder you are on yourself, the easier things become. Think of sacrifice in terms of benefits. Colvill's behavior demonstrated that sacrifice of self is the noblest way to influence.

Patriotism can motivate.

In spite of his willingness to bypass military rules, Colville had a strong sense of patriotism. Instead of having a romantic sentiment for his country, patriotism for Colville was a moral absolute. In effect, he repudiated the brand of patriotism that is defined as the last refuge of the scoundrel, a sometimes evangelistic manipulation of emotions used by leaders to hide or justify their evil intentions. His patriotism was developed over a lifetime of devotion to the principles he was called to save. From them he was able to draw strength to handle the deadly responsibility that awaited him on a moment's notice. Colville's value of patriotism allowed him to stand up to life's most stressful moment, the stark possibility of instant death. There can be no doubt that his patriotism was shared by both his own men and those who fought for the South. In an elemental sense, Colville, like so many men on the battlefield that day, may have seen himself as a humble guardian of a country that is one of laws and not of men, and that its protection truly required his life to be disposable. Devotion to this country's ideals - patriotism - can influence the kind of action that will continue to protect those ideals.

Your sacrifice makes a difference.

You live and work in small societies: family, neighbors and co-workers. What you sacrifice for the good of others can influence others to do the same. It could be suggested that William Colvill made only a tiny contribution not worth mentioning in the larger story of our country's history. To the contrary, like Colvill, you are a thread in the country's fabric, and you strengthen that fabric by your dedication to achievement. Without it, our country is weaker, and with it, our country is stronger, which is why it is impossible for you to be insignificant.

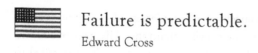

Failure is predictable.
Edward Cross

Cross was despised by many of his men for being a rough disciplinarian. He even threatened to shoot them personally if they attempted to "turn and run" during a battle. At least they gave him credit for keeping them well fed and clothed, which was no small feat in the daily rigors of war.

He was no stranger to a fight. Prior to Gettysburg, he traveled extensively to fight Indians in Arizona and survived two duels in Mexico. He came to Gettysburg with an inventory of eleven previous wounds. He had the habit of wearing a red bandanna into every fight, but in this battle he did something morbid and irregular: not only did he predict three times when and where he was going to die, but for the first time he put on a black bandanna to advertise his prediction. His nineteen-year-old assistant observed:

> Finally, the conversation turned on the impending struggle that we were hastening forward to, and at last the Colonel said, "It will be my last battle." He used the words in a grave decided way, and it gave me a shock, and also a feeling of resentment that he should speak in that manner; then I recalled to myself that in the last day or so he had at times seemed in a sort of abstracted mood that was not usual with him.
>
> At last he said to me; "... I wish you to attend to my books and papers; that private box of mine in the headquarters wagon; you helped me re-pack it the other day. After the campaign is over, get it at once, dry the contents if damp, and then turn it over to my brother Richard."

When General Hancock rode up to suggest there was an opportunity for Cross to be promoted to the rank of general, his response was immediate: "Too late, general, this is my last battle." Within hours he died from a mortal wound.

Cross was seen as a man of great courage and immeasurable fortitude. He executed his responsibilities in a calm and deliberate manner. But he sealed his fate by believing that he was doomed to die very soon. "I wished that I would live to see the rebellion suppressed and peace restored," he said as he drew his last breath, "...I think the boys will miss me. Say good-bye to all."

Gettysburg Lessons

Failure is predictable.

We all have the ability to determine when or how we are going to fail. Cross predicted on three occasions when he was going to die. The outcome of his prediction was no surprise. The influence of a negative thought leads to negative behavior that produces a negative result.

Success is predictable.

Since you are what you think, your actions will reflect what your mind is thinking. Moreover, if you decide you can do something, chances are very good that you will do it. Napoleon Hill said it best: "Whatever the mind can conceive and believe, it can achieve." Positive thinking is the primary influence that leads you to positive results.

Seize opportunity.

Gouverneur Warren

He was tactless, self-centered and opinionated. He had proven himself to be an excellent commander in previous battles. Now the chief engineer for the army under George Meade, he was trusted with military matters of the highest importance. Conscientious and thorough to a fault, he went to view the terrain on the left flank of the Union Army on the second day. What he discovered motivated him to make one of the more important command decisions of the battle.

Warren found the prize position all armies seek when looking to control the battlefield - high ground. He quickly concluded that a hill, known as Little Round Top, would serve as a great vantage point. "I was in such anxiety to get troops," Warren wrote later, that the "...discovery was intensely thrilling...and almost appalling."

After being slightly wounded by an exploding enemy artillery shell, he could see great numbers of Rebels partially hidden inside the tree line preparing to take the unoccupied hill. Urgently seeking to report what he had found and its strategic importance, he sent his aides to find Union troops to occupy the hill immediately. One of the aides was stopped by an officer who demanded to know his mission, and on discovery quickly ordered his own troops to take the hill. This action secured a key position for the Union during the second and third days of the battle.

Warren appreciated the importance of location in determining the value of the physical placement of troops. Since both armies had good troops capable of delivering good results, much of this battle would be determined by the army with the ideal location.

Gettysburg Lessons

Seize opportunity.

Do not wait for opportunity to come to you. Seek it out as Warren did. Most people live life wondering what their fortunes could have been if they had acted on their instincts to influence outcomes.

George Bernard Shaw was asked what he missed most about outliving kings, artists and philosophers he had known. His response was edifying: "What I miss most is the person I could have been."

Success often depends on your location.

Location can be where you place yourself on an issue. For example, when politicians are first to seize an issue they are perceived as originating and owning it, which results in a strategy that influences how people vote. Location is a strategy that allows you to provide something advantageous that competitors cannot duplicate.

To be first, be vigilant.

To be the first in any enterprise requires constant vigilance. Be first to assess opportunity, and first to respond to changing conditions. Warren proved, "Who's ever first... wins."

Take risks.
Strong Vincent

Gazing upon the Stars and Stripes, this twenty-six-year-old Harvard alumnus from Pennsylvania proclaimed with patriotic flare, "What death more glorious can any man desire than to die on the soil of old Pennsylvania fighting for that flag?"

He sensed an urgency to occupy a rocky hill. While waiting for orders to make his next move, he was told by a messenger that another officer would be told to take "that hill yonder." A senior Union officer on the staff of the commanding general had already determined its importance, but it appeared no Union forces were in readiness, or would not act quickly enough. Vincent determined that if his own men did not act soon, the Confederates would. Not waiting for orders, he commanded his men to take Little Round Top and declared he would take responsibility for reaching his own conclusion.

Knowing full well that taking action on his own was risking a court-martial, Vincent nevertheless felt compelled to take control. Communications with superiors were difficult at best, and there was no time to follow chain-of-command procedures. Military imperatives easily trumped protocol. His decision would be recorded as one of the many pivotal moments of the battle.

He was perceptive and swift in assessing the possible moves the Confederates would make on his position. Before his adversary could gain more ground, he hastily placed his troops where he expected attacks would occur. He ordered Joshua Lawrence Chamberlain of Maine to hold the very end of the Union line, a location that Chamberlain's men were convinced would not be attacked. Instructing Chamberlain to hold this position "at all hazards," Vincent directed his attention towards his own men until he was mortally wounded. His quick decision to take Little Round Top halted a possible setback. With his last words, "Don't give an inch!" his men held valuable ground. History wasted little time granting Vincent his most patriotic wish.

Gettysburg Lessons

Take risks.

Vincent's behavior reflects your ability to make quick and correct decisions in the face of great risk. Trust your instincts to overcome the fear of negative results. In early childhood someone told you every morning before going to school, "Be careful." You never heard that same person say, "Take some risks!" The safety of not failing is the greatest influence that will lead you to inaction and failure. Change your attitude to change your results; the glass is always half full.

Think for yourself.

Under the pressure of time, Vincent did not let rules get in the way. He saw an opportunity that influenced him to get the job done. His moment of truth was ignoring his superiors to solve a problem that demanded immediate attention. Organizations and bureaucracies often do not react quickly enough in a fast-paced environment, but individuals can react fast at any level to get results. Results are as likely to come from the bottom as from the top.

Be tough on yourself.

Whatever yardstick you use to measure success, don't give an inch! The easier you are on yourself the more difficult you will find life's challenges. The harder you are on yourself the more readily you will attain your aspirations. Good leadership is tough-on-yourself leadership.

A good team outperforms an individual.

With urgency Vincent had to rely on his men, a team of individuals working together for the same purpose. Results and leadership by each person's influence must be encouraged to come from all levels, not just from the top. A cohesive group simply accomplishes more than an individual acting alone.

Despite limitations you can succeed.

Joshua Lawrence Chamberlain

Unlike many Union generals, Chamberlain had no military training. Fluent in several languages and a college professor of logic and natural theology, he possessed a simple resolve to play a small role in keeping the Union together. As secession became a reality, he wrote passionately that it "was war upon the Union; and that meant the destruction of the United States — body, life and being." When it appeared that he was about to die from a horrible wound, he was the only Union officer in the Civil War to receive a battlefield promotion to general.

In the habit of visualizing what his adversary might do, he would mentally prepare a strategy to meet the challenge. This mental technique dated back to his days as a college student when he struggled with his first adversary, which was his own speech impediment of stuttering. To succeed at what you want to do, he wrote, "...feel the emotion of it [accomplishment], and that will bear you to its motion." In other words, experience the feelings of what you visualize and achievement will be set in motion. Not surprisingly he became an accomplished speaker.

Positive traits that would prove productive were his senses of fairness and persuasiveness. Just before the battle he was given a unit of belligerent Maine veterans who were in no mood to cooperate. Chamberlain had the option to treat them as prisoners preparatory to a court-martial for desertion. Instead, he initiated a relationship by distributing food while discussing what needed to be done. He communicated his vision in such a way that they became clear on his objective. By winning their confidence he now had the crucial number of fighting men necessary to carry out the next operation. But pressure was mounting fast.

Improvisation, another talent, came at the most critical moment. On the second day of battle Chamberlain's regiment, exhausted and nearly surrounded, ran out of ammunition. In a position that he was ordered to hold "at all hazards," he stood at the very brink of disaster. He could surrender the end of the Union line, or he could fix bayonets and make a last ditch effort to hold his position. There was no choice, his orders were crystal clear: "at all hazards" was to be taken literally. He had to think quickly as to how he was going to stand firm with his men.

He did not order a charge. "It was vain," he later wrote, "to order 'Forward'." He put a charge in motion simply by screaming the word, "Bayonets!" "There are things," he added, 'whose seed is in itself.'" A commander was entitled to take credit for the actions of his men, yet he insisted for years after the event that his men were more deserving of credit on the second day. Nevertheless, the War Department cited him for bravery and awarded him the Medal of Honor.

Gettysburg Lessons

Despite limitations you can succeed.

With limited resources you can still get the job done, influence others to act by simply saying a single word. When Chamberlain yelled "Bayonets!" after his men had run out of ammunition, this one word led them to charge ahead. They quickly discovered that their resources were not so limited after all. If you cannot find your calculator, use a pencil; if you cannot exercise by running, try walking; if you cannot find a teaching job, try mentoring; if you cannot do a project all by yourself, ask for help.

Use your imagination.

Twenty-five years after the battle, Chamberlain wrote of imagination as the force that "enables men to do things they did not dream themselves capable of before..." Albert Einstein echoed Chamberlain many years later: "Imagination can go places where knowledge cannot." Succeed by using your imagination. It can help you unleash unknown resources. It gives you the advantage to improvise on what you already have. It can provide the one answer you need. It is the mind's back-up mechanism when all else fails. To "get" imagination, sit quietly, close your eyes and imagine the joy you are experiencing by having accomplished your goal. Then feel the excitement as if you already achieved your objective. Or, brainstorm with others to discover a workable idea, and the excitement of that discovery will influence you to find your solution.

Motivate by giving credit.

Give full credit to others when they contribute to your achievement; you will gain their respect. Recognition can also translate into someone else's dedication to your objectives. You are leading others to productivity by the influence of your positive words and actions.

Communicating your vision gets results.

Do not be surprised when subordinates act in a positive manner independently of you. What they are doing is anticipating you, instinctively aware of what you want them to do. You have effectively communicated your vision of where you want them to go. You have led them by the influence of your purpose. Their experience of your trust encourages them to exercise their own judgment, responsibilities and talents. The "seed [of productivity] is in itself." If your organization is expanding, chances are you are being anticipated, somebody is already working on your expansion plans.

To realize a goal, first visualize it.

Visualizing and feeling terrific - "to feel the emotion of it" - about the outcome will assure better results. Improve job performance by visualizing the raise you seek, better grades by visualizing the scores you want, better health by visualizing the trim body you desire, and improved relationships by visualizing yourself with positive and uplifting people. Your visualizations will influence you to act in your own best interests. Every four years this technique receives much publicity during the Olympic Games.

Be certain you are understood.

When Chamberlain was told to hold his line "at all hazards," the instruction was absolutely clear. Because he was able to communicate orders to his men without confusion or ambiguity, instructions were not misunderstood and victory was achieved. A powerful influence is a simple communication.

The like-minded achieve goals.

Sam Keene

He had a family and a thriving law practice. Men younger than he were available to do the fighting, but there was one problem that continued to disturb him: he was convinced that army management was in the hands of grossly incompetent people who were wastefully spending young lives. He believed his country was in desperate need of educated and successful men who could contribute their talents and experience to manage the war and bring it to a speedy conclusion. He set off to recruit similarly thinking men and became the leader of his own unit.

Patriotism was driving his efforts to recruit, and the cynicism he felt about the administration of the war was shared by those he recruited. Keene and his Maine men were under no illusion that they could change the army. Perhaps it was a shared belief that they could make a difference, but they could not stand by and allow the old men in Washington to continue making what they regarded as a mess of the war.

What he and his men did not expect was their commitment to influence the outcome would have an affect, albeit small, on American history, all stemming from a single action that would last for less than two hours. He and his men were part of the 20th Maine regiment under Joshua Lawrence Chamberlain that assisted in a pivotal moment of the battle. When Keene was wounded in the hip, he never expressed the cynicism he had when he joined the army. Perhaps his instincts told him that he and his men did make a difference. They managed the war themselves in a very limited but vital way they could not have predicted.

Gettysburg Lessons

The like-minded achieve goals.

When you are part of a truly cohesive team, one of shared and powerful interests, you can be up against seemingly insurmountable odds and succeed. Each team member influences other members. Sam Keene and Martin Luther King, Jr. were supported by like-minded people who believed as they did. King accomplished landmark civil rights legislation that had no hope of passing a few years earlier. Likewise, low income inner-city housing projects, often havens for criminals, have successfully brought their occupants together in a community effort with law enforcement to eliminate unwanted elements. This is group empowerment, power that comes from influencing each other towards an achievable goal.

Do what you ought to do.

Charles Knapp

Having seen so much death, mutilation, amputation, sickness and disease, he was anxious to go home to his family and live a normal life. He had joined the army for three years, but ended up in another unit whose two-year obligation had expired just weeks before the great battle. He refused an order to finish his own three-year requirement. Along with many other men he felt release from duty should be granted simply because he had seen enough of war, regardless of what his enlistment papers said. Perhaps he also rationalized that life was unfair, or that war forced boys to become men too quickly. In Knapp's mind his fighting days were over. He was placed under arrest, but his fate changed when he was assigned to the command of Joshua Lawrence Chamberlain, who would become Gettysburg's most famous soldier.

Demoralized and reluctant to pick up his musket again, he had to find an answer to the most elemental question, "What's in it for me?" To continue fighting he would be confronted with carrot-and-stick motivation: the stick was either facing a firing squad, or imprisonment for desertion. In close-knit nineteenth century communities, the carrot was returning home and being recognized for performing honorably. Moreover, it is doubtful that his decision to fight was generated by some philosophical ideal. Presumably he decided to go along with Chamberlain because it simply meant his survival, or at the very least, saving face with the folks back home. Had not Knapp's own interests been satisfied that day, Chamberlain may not have succeeded in holding his ground.

Gettysburg Lessons

Do what you ought to do.

Life is a creative tension between "what's in it for me?" and what you ought to do, between what you know and what you ought to know, between what you think and what you ought to think, between what you accept and what you ought to fight for. Freedom beckons you to do what you want to do, but responsibility tells you what you ought to do. Success is the union of the freedom to exercise your talents and the

127

responsibility to use those talents wisely. Doing what you ought to do is the ideal influence.

To produce change, appeal to self-interest.

People will not change unless you satisfy their self-interests. They want to know how they are going to benefit personally from your recommendations, directives, suggestions, or orders. A personal gain must be obvious. This is the point where the roles of leader and follower switch. Leadership, instead of being a stimulus-response experience, is now response-stimulus: the follower influences the leader, just as Knapp influenced Chamberlain. Achieve a gain and, like Chamberlain, you will follow another's influence and achieve what you both want. Nations imitate Knapp: they are driven by interests, not by ideals.

Incentives work providing they are commensurate with the change being sought. Some people will not change if your purpose is in direct conflict with their aims, or if the reason for change is unreasonable. You will not produce the same results if your earnings are reduced. You will not always do additional school work if extra credit is not offered. You will not go on a diet if higher self-esteem is not the result. In other words, you will not work towards a goal if there is no perceived personal benefit.

A little can mean a lot.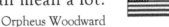
Orpheus Woodward

High ground was the highest-priced real estate in battle. Possession was nine-tenths of the law for victory. Woodward was in charge of an infantry regiment that joined forces with three others. Their task was to keep the Confederates from occupying an important hill.

Woodward observed that one particular unit to the immediate left of his position was taking more casualties under repeated attacks, was running out of ammunition, and was on the brink of being overtaken. He sensed that unless he stretched his own line farther to his left, the entire hill would be lost.

By this simple act of extending his own line, Woodward made it possible for the commander of the other regiment to stretch his, thus keeping the hill in Union hands. Woodward's observation was surprisingly modest, as if to indicate that his action was insignificant: "The contest continued lively," he wrote later, "until nearly 6 p.m., when the enemy fell back." The commander whose unit was desperate for assistance, and to this day receives all the credit for holding the hill, expressed a debt of gratitude to Woodward whose "cooperation made his movements conform to my necessities, so my right was at no time exposed to flank attack." The comments were made by the commander who years later became the most famous citizen-soldier of the Civil War, Joshua Lawrence Chamberlain.

Gettysburg Lessons

A little can mean a lot.

When a winning team is suddenly in need of help, one person's action can keep the team from losing. Woodward proved that a seemingly insignificant decision can lead a team to a great victory.

Balance enthusiasm with responsibility.
William Barksdale

He could qualify as the best coach in the National Football League. A highly aggressive and proud man from Mississippi, he declared that he had "never been whipped and never can be." A former newspaper editor and congressman with a silver tongue for oratory, he gave inspiring speeches to his men who made up one of the best fighting units in the war. Overly anxious to make a charge in battle and utterly convinced that he could decimate the enemy in five minutes, he was frustrated with an order to wait. That his enemy had a stronger position did not matter. Convinced of success he was emotionally and mentally prepared to demonstrate his desire to achieve it.

When finally given the order to advance, one of his captains observed that Barksdale's face became "radiant with joy." While his attack was in motion, one Union officer would later remark that "it was the grandest charge that was ever made by mortal man." He refused to retreat even when opposing fire was ripping holes in his own line. Urged to halt and regroup, he yelled, "No!...we have [the enemy] on the run." It was vintage Barksdale, encouraging his men with his own optimism in the very heat of battle: "Brave Mississippians, one more charge and the day is ours!" After using only 4 regiments to whip more than 10 of the enemy's, his next charge was pushing his luck a little too far.

With unfettered zeal and a ballooning sense of his own prowess, his long white hair simply drew too much attention. While shot in his saddle and in the confusion that followed, he was presumed dead and left on the field. He was captured by Union soldiers and taken to the rear. Defiant to the end, he knew that the only fight left in him was what he could discharge verbally, the kind he demonstrated so well in the halls of Congress. Perhaps he was duty-bound to utter his last words in a final burst of bravado: "Beware! You [Yankees] will have [Confederate General] Longstreet thundering in your rear in the morning!" Warrior William Barksdale would not be whipped.

Gettysburg Lessons

Balance enthusiasm with responsibility.

Barksdale had the vision of an independent South to inspire and motivate his men. They internalized his vision - led by his influence - and fought successfully against all odds. But you cannot win at anything if you choose to be unaware of potential problems. Like Barksdale you cannot win against an opponent if all you have is vision and excitement. You cannot expect something positive to happen unless you are prepared to spend the time, personal energy, and the proper amount of resources to justify your enthusiasm.

Good followers reflect good leaders.

Soldiers are often as good as their commander wants them to be, as players are with their coach, students with their teacher, children with their parents, and employees with their employer. People in leadership positions, who encourage achievement, usually see positive results. People in followship positions, who see results, are easily led. It is no wonder that an encouraging word is good leadership verbalized.

Allow failure to harden your resolve.
George Willard

Against the wishes of his parents he joined the army at eighteen. His remarkable military family included generals in the Revolutionary War and the War of 1812. As a superior soldier he was often promoted, and by 1861 he was the captain of his own regiment. Before Gettysburg he was made a colonel of a New York volunteer group.

Military standards of failure could exact a cruel judgment against an officer in spite of his best efforts to avoid it. If captured, he brought shame upon himself until he could prove competency and bravery in battle. Ten months earlier, Willard and his men were so inexperienced that they were captured at Harper's Ferry by Mississippi and South Carolina forces. After his release in a prisoner exchange, his senior officers were scrutinizing his every move. His men were derided with the epithet, "The Harper's Ferry Brigade." Spending seven months on leave at an army camp, his men were drilled daily in preparation for reclaiming their honor. He was going to make real soldiers of these novices, or die trying.

On the second day, with one of many gaps that had opened in the Union line, Union General Hays gave Willard his last order: "Take your brigade over there and knock the hell out of the rebs!" Willard shouted, "Fix bayonets!" It did not go unnoticed that his men were well-drilled. With no support Willard's men went forward to carry out their orders and win back their reputation. It was all or nothing.

With the summer sun pushing temperatures to eighty degrees, Willard's soldiers went forward hungry, fatigued, but unwavering. One of his men later recalled that Willard "lined us up as if we were on parade instead of under a perfect storm of missiles from mini balls to busting shells." Soon his line was being broken by a group of retreating Union soldiers, perhaps unnerving his own men who needed to prove themselves. With hearts pounding rapidly and bladders expelling their contents, they marched directly toward an oncoming enemy shouting, "Remember Harper's Ferry!" Willard drove the Confederates into retreat with enough time to recapture some Union artillery pieces. An incredible irony was making its appearance: the retreating Confederates under General Barksdale were the same forces that captured Willard and his men at Harper's Ferry ten months earlier. With Barksdale mortally wounded in this latest engagement, the action of Willard's men and their leader quickly erased any suspicions of their courage. Their redemption had finally arrived, but Willard's fate was short-lived. On his way back to the rear, he was killed by a shell fragment that tore away the front half of his head.

Gettysburg Lessons

Allow failure to harden your resolve.

Failure is success turned inside out: you can turn failure into success just as Willard did. Allow failure to influence you to be better prepared, knowing what not to do next time. Willard's story demonstrates that what counts is not what happens to you, but how you respond to what happens to you. Your most empowering freedom is your ability to choose your attitude - an energizing influence that leads you to better outcomes.

Emphasize training, not just education.

Willard spent a great deal of time drilling his men in a competency that was needed to achieve results. Training how to hold, carry, load and shoot a rifle was more important than knowing the history, mechanics and purpose of rifles. The influence of training, not education, won the fight.

Use the Golden Rule.
Louis Francine

He came from a French family with a two-hundred-year history of knights, counts, and military men. After his father moved the family to New Jersey, he had his fourteen-year-old son continue his education in Paris, later matriculating to a government school for officers in the French army. Learning social graces with a countess who was his aunt, Louis became an attractive and affable young man. He now enjoyed the image of a scholar and a gentleman. In 1858, he returned to his New Jersey home, and by the outbreak of the war he seemed destined for a leadership role. He was selected to be captain of his own regiment.

With the admiration and great respect of his men, he was described by one of his sergeants in a New Jersey newspaper: "Our boys are in perfect love with him, and will follow him through 'thick and thin'...Capt. Francine will leave his mark." In two separate instances that were highly unusual during the war, when two higher officer positions became vacant, petitions from his own men were signed so that Francine could be promoted. One petition read that a promotion was "due to him for his untiring efforts towards promoting the efficiency and discipline of the regiment." Within his own ranks this impressive captain became a colonel by petition, practically unheard of in the annals of war. The fact remains that he made his men models of precision and drill, a discipline that would serve them well in the days ahead.

At Gettysburg Francine's regiment was ordered to support an artillery battery that was already dueling with a Rebel unit. With no cover and no place to go under intense fire, Francine ordered his men to hug the ground with no way to escape the terror of the moment. With enemy shells making direct hits, dismembered bodies started to populate quickly. Francine had no alternative but to order a retreat. He was stopped by a general's aid, reminding him that he had to hold his position at all costs since his men were "doing fine execution." His immediate response: "I was only trying to get a better position for my men, who I am losing very fast."

Confusion was killing the notion of making a last stand. More Rebels were pouring in on a hopelessly vulnerable Union position. Colonel Francine ordered his men to fix bayonets and make a desperate charge, but it was too late. In a matter of minutes, half of his men were either dead or wounded. Francine received a severe wound to the thigh, which would prove mortal two weeks later.

Within a year his father died after being so stricken with grief. The very men who petitioned to have their leader promoted convened a meeting a month later to commemorate his death with these words:

Resolved, That we...feel deeply the loss of one who by his many acts of kindness, and who, as a soldier, friend, and gentleman had won our highest esteem and regard.

Gettysburg Lessons

Use the Golden Rule.
The best leader can be the one who practices the Golden Rule. Understand, trust, respect, and above all, appreciate your followers as Francine did. As a group their positive responses will influence you to continue your positive behavior. Treat others as you would like others to treat you, and you can influence a person, a team, or an army to do just about anything.

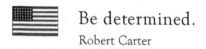

Be determined.

Robert Carter

He refused to be distracted from an annoying little infirmity that would have defeated most able-bodied men. He was not suffering bullet or shell fragment wounds. He was in constant pain from blisters as a result of wearing undersized shoes, going barefoot, and marching nearly seventy miles. To make matters worse, his feet started bleeding just two miles from Gettysburg. So what really carried him to his destination? He could have been motivated by the threat of being court-martialed for desertion, but there is no record or entry in his diary of any such threat. The pain of bleeding feet was nothing compared to being labeled by his fellow hometown soldiers as a quitter, or a coward. The wrong label was motivation enough.

He later wrote that during war there was "a slight tendency to doubt oneself, when the bullets buzzed so closely by without touching some part of the body,..." What did he mean exactly? Was death teasing him? It was. Was the thought of death, being so close at hand, creating serious doubt that he would live through this ghastly horror? It did. Under these horrific circumstances, self-doubt was real and expected. Yet during the Civil War it was typical to write of one's feelings in almost neutral terms so as not to give away feelings of vulnerability, or cowardice.

There was a moment when history seemed to ordain Carter as an angel of mercy. After a day's fighting, he surveyed an area where many of the dead, dying and wounded of Lee's army still lay. He was completely surrounded by the sights and sounds of misery. At one point, he observed a Confederate officer attempting to stop the flow of blood from a leg wound. Troubled by the sight, he rose to approach the dying man and offered him a canteen of water. Looking up, the Rebel thanked him for his merciful gesture. Carter's appearance must have given the officer cause to wonder: this enemy soldier looked too young to be a killer, he's just a boy! Before long the two were engaged in a conversation about the battle's progress.

Their meeting prompted a spontaneous camaraderie, presumably a shared influence on each other that neither could have predicted. One was led by the other to be merciful, and the other was led to accept mercy. Such meetings were not uncommon in the Civil War.

Years later Carter wrote what must be the most graphic account of the physical results of battle:

> ...Corpses strewed the ground at every step. Arms, legs, heads, and parts of dismembered bodies were scattered about, and sticking among the rocks, and against the trunks of trees, hair, brains, and entrails and shreds of human flesh still hung...

War dismantled any structure of youthful idealism and forced an unwelcome realism on a young Carter who left Gettysburg as a man at the age of seventeen.

Gettysburg Lessons

Be determined.

Determination is self-motivation, an attitude that propels you toward a destination not hampered by limitations of the body. Mental barriers, not physical ones, will always prevent you from achieving your goals. Carter's attitude would not allow physical impediments to get in the way of reaching his final destination. Attitude for Carter had its foundation in honor and courage, doing the right thing at risk to his own life.

Face your problems head-on.

The odds may seem overwhelming, but wheelchair athletes "run" in marathons and paraplegics operate computers with their jaws. Face your problems head-on, and work diligently to find solutions. You may have Carter's feet, with determination to reach a more positive position in your life. Begin by planning the small steps you must take, one at a time. These are the influences that will lead you to your own destination. Acknowledge that you will get some blisters along the way, but you can be a young Carter who never loses faith in your ability to reach your objective.

Elevate your motivations.
Paul Revere

It was legal to pay someone three hundred dollars (approximately five thousand in today's dollars) to fight in one's place. Some had relatives of social status; others knew someone of prominence who could keep them out of harm's way. Although patriotism was a strong sentiment, it was nonetheless easy for someone of historical lineage to remain uncommitted. Not so for Paul Revere, who was a descendent of the famous Revolutionary War patriot. Revere took action not only to further honor his famous family name, but also to preserve his country. Understandably his mother resisted his decision. To her he responded:

> I have weighed it all and there is something higher still. The institutions of the country, indeed free institutions throughout the world, hang on this moment.... I should be ashamed of myself if I were to sit down in happy indulgence, and leave such a great matter as this to take its course.... I will never go without your consent; but I shall be humbled if I stay at home.

With great reluctance she consented, but she would not have to wait long to learn how far her son was prepared to go for his country. On July 2, thirty-year-old Colonel Paul Revere was mortally wounded by Confederate artillery fire. History proved him right, that his life was spent for the "institutions of the country" that endure to this day.

His willing consent to fight, motivated by his love for freedom and his country, perpetuated his famous last name.

Gettysburg Lessons

Elevate your motivations.

Pursue ideals and be a role model who leads by the influence of your behavior. This was Revere's legacy, and it can be yours. Your education, wealth, or good name will have greater meaning as you use them to benefit others as well as yourself.

Trust your instincts.

Freeman McGilvery

McGilvery's senior officer referred to him as the "cool clear headed old sailor" from Maine. As an artillery commander who had to make quick decisions on the second day, his cannon positions were about to be overrun by a large force of Confederate infantry.

A gap had opened in the Union position, and a new line of defense had to be established. The only resources available were the battered remnants of his units. It was a desperate situation requiring equally desperate measures. McGilvery approached one of his officers and gave an order that may well be one of the most terrifying ever received by a subordinate commander in the history of warfare:

> ...you must remain where you are and hold your position at all hazards, and *sacrifice your battery, if need be*, until at least I can find some batteries to put in position and cover you.

McGilvery wasted no time in riding a short distance and removing cannons from other artillery units, even though he had no authority to do so. He then positioned these cannons along a line of woods while deceiving the enemy into thinking that he had plenty of infantry support. This caused the Confederates to hesitate. "I ordered canister [fire] to be used on the low bushes in front, which compelled them to retire." Support troops arrived in the nick of time to hold the Union line.

McGilvery's quick thinking under extreme pressure, with no regard for his own safety or career, saved a seemingly hopeless situation.

Gettysburg Lessons

Trust your instincts.

Trust them to solve problems. McGilvery's instincts helped solve his problem. Under intense pressure, McGilvery proved that your mental abilities can work at lightening speed. Your mind is able to bring together a lifetime of related experiences in microseconds, discharging data for making good decisions quickly. Delaying decisions when all the facts are fresh in your mind is cheating yourself of making an informed decision. Fresh facts are influences you can trust.

Manage your time.

Pressure forced McGilvery to manage his time efficiently. When you find yourself under great stress, prioritize your tasks and concentrate on what has to be done first. High-pressure situations demand that you be more organized. Make time-management a part of your daily routine. Ask yourself a question that may have been hounding McGilvery at every turn: "What is the best use of my time at this very moment?" Asking this question everyday is a powerful management influence that will lead you to make good decisions.

Go above and beyond.

Refusing to do something that is not called for in your job description may harm your career. But McGilvery proved that under extraordinary conditions, going above and beyond your duties with personal initiative can be rewarding. Initiative also springs from a goal that influences desired outcomes.

Discipline yourself to succeed.

John Bigelow

He was first in his Harvard class to enlist in the army in 1861. His youth and inexperience convinced him to rely on one element of command that was required of new recruits: discipline. Enlistees came to the war with various attitudes. Some wanted adventure because they were bored, others wanted to fight for a cause. No one ever expected that Bigelow's orders would require his men to do difficult and tediously repetitive actions, the kind that prepare soldiers for the most stressful moments of combat. At one point in their training, not atypical of what new recruits think of their officers, his bugler wrote: "He is worse than any regular [soldier] that ever breathed."

On July 2, Bigelow's small artillery group was nearly surrounded. The moment was desperate. The Union line was broken and a huge gap was opening. The Confederate juggernaut could plow through at any moment. The enemy had advanced to within three hundred feet. "I was alone on the field," he later recounted, "without supports of any kind." Instructed by his commander to hold his position "at all hazards," and "sacrifice your battery, if need be," Bigelow directed a retreat calculated to slow down the enemy advance. He was buying time to save an army.

At least forty-five horses, harnessed to haul heavy cannons, were shot down. He had to resort to pulling his available cannons by hand and continue firing while moving, which was an almost impossible task. Bigelow recalled that "Sergeant after sergt. was struck down...bullets now came in on all sides....The air was dark with smoke.... The enemy [was] yelling like demons, yet my men kept up a rapid fire..." With the Confederates continuing to press hard and fast, he had no other choice but to stop firing and order his men to pull out immediately.

Bigelow was shot from his horse, and despite his heroic pleas to be left behind, his bugler placed him back on another mount. He was now between the Confederate line of attack and the new Union line of artillery that had just been formed by his superior. He was in no-man's land with more than two hundred yards left before he could reach the relative safety of the new Union line.

Bullets were still flying and shells were bursting everywhere. Told by a junior officer to hurry so that the Union batteries could commence firing, "I told him to fire away," Bigelow wrote, "I could not hurry." Still bleeding and trying to avoid more pain from bouncing on a running horse, both he and his bugler decided that walking the horse was a better idea.

For chivalrous reasons he was never fired on again when Confederate soldiers could have easily killed him (It was not uncommon in the Civil War for the opposition to withhold firing at a soldier who displayed unusual bravery). He later recognized that the disciplined performance of his men "delayed the enemy 30 precious minutes," which successfully held off a Rebel advance. It was just long enough to close a gap in the Union line.

One captured Confederate said later to Bigelow's survivors, "Never saw such men; you didn't know when you were whipped...."

Like so many other pivotal moments in the battle, the Union line was saved because precious time was purchased with bravery, sacrifice, and above all, discipline. Months earlier, Bigelow had drilled his men constantly so that when the moment arrived, they would have the discipline to do exactly what they were told. With Bigelow's leadership they were able to stave off an overwhelming and determined enemy. The last words in the official report by his commander, Freeman McGilvery, amounted to a commander's honoring salute: "...Bigelow's conduct was gallant in the extreme." If discipline is the maintenance drug of leadership, Bigelow was energized to fight his next battle.

Gettysburg Lessons

Discipline yourself to succeed.

Even though Bigelow's men were inexperienced, the discipline they demonstrated on that day allowed them to withstand overwhelming odds. Despite inexperience, discipline gives you the focus to get the job done. Success requires it. You cannot expect good results in any endeavor unless you exercise discipline to avoid the distractions of everyday living. The very display of discipline is influential - you signal the behavior needed to achieve results.

Trust your instincts.

When you are forced to make decisions "without supports of any kind," you can make good ones by trusting your instincts. They will lead you to concentrate your energies in the direction you want to go. You will think of strategies to use and resources to tap.

You are a leader.

You lead as soon as you influence one person or yourself to take any action, or no action. To define a leader as someone in charge of a group on a mission is too restrictive since it ignores everyone's innate ability to influence. Because you already influence either by example, word, or thought, you are a leader. The most powerful example of leadership is a parent.

Success is in the preparation.

George Greene

He was a leader who accomplished so much in so little time, yet there was so little written about him. Like so many who survived to fight another battle, he was a stealth commander: he did not make himself a target on a horse, did not make a famous statement, did not lead a celebrated charge, did not have a high casualty rate, and by the medical standards of the day, he was an old man at sixty-two. Mature enough to avoid the seductions of glory, he met none of the standard requirements for special recognition or fame. As luck would have it, an inexplicable omission of his name from his superior's official report of the battle guaranteed George Greene's anonymity for one hundred and forty years.

Greene taught engineering and mathematics at West Point for thirteen years. At age thirty-five, after resigning from his teaching position, he went on to be a civil engineer and worked in railroad construction for several years. Employed by the city's water department, he was building a reservoir in New York City's Central Park. He reentered the army as a colonel to lead a group of New York volunteers.

On July 2, George Greene calmly instructed his men on how to prepare for a headlong attack. He had them cut down trees and build walls for defense, though no enemy was in sight. There was no clear indication early that day that a fight was going to take place at his location, but Greene was the walking and talking embodiment of the Boy Scout motto, "Be Prepared." Late in the day the battle for Culp's Hill began, and Greene found himself outnumbered five to one. But he was impregnably positioned.

Part of his strategy was to keep his regiments rotated to insure an ample supply of ammunition and to minimize fatigue. "The value of this defense," he recalled after the battle, "was shown in our subsequent operations by our small loss compared with that of...a vastly superior force." He succeeded in keeping his cool, keeping the hill, and keeping a low profile. One officer later declared that "...the noble veteran Greene, by his resistance against overwhelming odds...saved the army."

Unlike some generals who sought a high profile for heroics real or alleged, Greene never uttered a word of complaint about not receiving his due credit. What mattered was that he did his duty, finished his job, and had the satisfaction of giving credit, not to himself, but to his men. One of the last remarks in his official report of the battle was characteristic: "...my thanks are due for their gallantry and great activity during this contest as at all other times."

He has the postwar distinction of being Gettysburg's only officer to be buried in his home state of Rhode Island under a 2-ton rock from Culp's Hill.

Gettysburg Lessons

Success is in the preparation.

Greene instructs us to prepare for the expected and the unexpected. Being prepared is influencing yourself and others on the way to a favorable outcome in any endeavor.

Satisfaction comes from within.

Deriving satisfaction from what you finish does not require the whole world to know about it. This is how Greene approached his duties. If you think the rest of the world does not notice what you accomplish, think again. Your actions may not be recognized with a trophy, a congratulatory memo, or a luncheon of tribute, but you will influence people who will copy the good that you do.

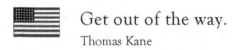

Get out of the way.

Thomas Kane

Before the Civil War this humanitarian did much to help the Mormons of Utah avoid violent confrontations with the US government. He never became a Mormon, but affection for him resulted in a statue of his likeness as one of only two to be displayed today in the state house in Salt Lake City.

Like his Southern counterpart, Johnston Pettigrew, he was one of the most cultured and educated men of his time. The son of a federal judge in Philadelphia, Kane learned the law from his father after a period of study in Paris. Subsequent to accepting a federal job as a US commissioner, he resigned his position in protest, refusing to enforce the Fugitive Slave Act that required federal officials to return fugitive slaves to their owners. His own father had him arrested and thrown in jail for contempt. Eventually freed, he dedicated much of his time to helping slaves escape on the Underground Railroad.

When the war started, he recruited hearty men from the backwoods of Pennsylvania. Contrary to the gruff image of an officer, he never hesitated to use an umbrella for shade while drilling them. A free thinker not given to following standard military rules, he insisted on the uncommon and unrequired activity of target practice to develop sharpshooters of his men. He would later name his unit the "Bucktails," because they wore part of a deer's tail on their caps.

Having been shot in the face and leg in prior battles, and severely bruised by a rifle butt to the chest, he was ill enough to finally leave the army. Yet when he learned there was going to be a major engagement in his home State, he struggled from his sickbed, disguised himself as a citizen to avoid capture, and ventured back to his old command. Courage left him completely resistant to rest and recuperation.

When he arrived in Gettysburg in an ambulance wagon at 6 a.m. on July 2, he became sick with pneumonia. He soon realized he could not command and must step aside. He could have withdrawn to the protective shelter of a field hospital, but when the bullets started flying he kept his head down and stayed ready to offer advice to the officer in charge.

Kane suffered with his diminished physical capacity, but his good sense gave dignity and honor to the word "advisor," not to mention that he was giving courage its finest exhibit. Most importantly, he defined a "hero" as someone who ought to do the right thing in the face of extraordinary adversity. Out of necessity and with grace, he gave up his authority that day while becoming his country's ideal American, Citizen Kane.

Gettysburg Lessons

Get out of the way.

Take yourself out of the lead position if you become a hindrance to the success of the team. To remain an asset and functional, get out of the way and allow others to tap into their own experiences and knowledge. Like Kane, assign authority to someone else if you do not want to lose involvement. Effective managing is directing others to do what you are unable to do. To lead is to trust individuals or teammates to use their talents for their benefit and yours. As a contemporary equivalent of Kane, Lee Iacocca once remarked, "I hire people brighter than me and then I get out of their way."

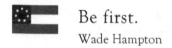

Be first.
Wade Hampton

He knew how to manage people and identified an opportunity when he saw it. By the time the war began, he was one of the wealthiest plantation owners in the South as well as a US Senator. Perhaps to protect his vast interests, he joined the cause of the South and put his talents to work immediately.

In one bright shining moment of battle, he suspended the adage, "All's fair in love and war." He wanted to fight fairly with a young Union soldier who had just fired two shots that barely missed him. Hampton returned his fire, but also missed his target. From a distance, it appeared that the young man was either short on ammunition, or slow to reload. Without the protection of any junior officers, Hampton rode alone to get closer to his opponent. In effect, he was now initiating what may have been the Gettysburg campaign's only duel, an isolated exchange of gunfire between two men.

In need of reloading, his young adversary waved his hand as if to say, "Just gimme a minute! I'll get back to ya!" As if his honor required it, Hampton paused. Losing patience after two attempts to hit each other at a little more than one hundred yards, Hampton had waited long enough. He raised his pistol and shot the young man, wounding him in the wrist. His solitary act of waiting ended in his adversary running off into the protection of the woods. At this instant Hampton received a surprise blow to the back of his head from a sword brandished from a mounted Union cavalryman. The bleeding Hampton turned and chased his foe, but after his pistol continued to misfire at close range, he finally threw it at his target. Hampton's frustration triggered a well-aimed and full-throated blast of all the profanity he could muster.

Gettysburg Lessons

Be first.

In a competitive environment, you cannot wait for your competitor to make the first move. Your moves must be pre-emptive in order to stop your competitor from challenging you effectively. Once you establish a pattern of "firsts," potential customers will think of you first when they are ready to do business. IBM had the reputation of coming out first with new products and then forced those products into obsolescence by creating the "new and improved." It forced competitors to surrender trying to compete, and an industry developed around the IBM technology. IBM was an industry standard of influence by being first. To stay ahead in making computer chips, INTEL doubles its microprocessor chip speed with regularity. When you are first consistently, your chances for success are always greater because it reflects proper planning and innovation.

Never act alone needlessly.

When possible, do not go into a challenging situation alone as Hampton did. Find talented people who can help you succeed. They will influence you by offering innovative suggestions you may not have considered. Even when you think you have the know-how to complete a project of any kind by yourself, think again. Going solo is fine when you are bowling, but when you are on a team, let team members make suggestions. Someone else might have a better idea.

Have an alternative strategy.

John Bell Hood

"Old Wooden Head" was a master of the blunt and brief. In a previous battle he was asked the whereabouts of his division. "Dead on the field," was his reply. The nephew of a US congressman, he entered West Point and, like his commander James Longstreet, graduated near the bottom of his class. He rose in the military ranks by proven tactical performances on the field. But he was not known for being logical. He was "inclined to be impetuous in his decisions, trust in his intuition and his blind optimism to see him through." A female observer described him as having a "sad face" and "an appearance of awkward strength."

After being ordered to make an attack up a road in the direction of the town of Gettysburg, Hood pleaded for what he believed was a disaster-proof alternative, which was to swing around the undefended southern side of a nearby mountain. He was denied three times, and each time he proposed the exact same plan. He was unquestionably frustrated and protested the orders of a superior officer for the first time in his military career, with the added conviction that following orders would turn his right flank and rear into a dangerous shooting gallery. He faced a new enemy he could not defeat: a superior's deaf ear.

Hood's attack became a diversion, which he concluded was demanded by the tactical situation, but it was not in conformity with the original attack plan.

Hood's attack met unforeseen resistance. He was personally hit with a shell fragment and was put out of commission for the rest of the battle. His men were now deprived of a senior officer to direct their movements and would soon meet defeat. "I shall ever believe," still defending his plan in a letter he wrote thirteen years later, "that had I been permitted to turn Round Top Mountain, we would not only have gained that position, but have been able finally to rout the enemy."

Gettysburg Lessons

Have an alternative strategy.

The certainty of your position can be as seductive as it was for Hood. You may be so excited for your plan's success that you fail to consider alternative moves in the event of unforeseen circumstances. Murphy's Law is a constant: if something will go wrong, it will. Design your success plan with at least one back-up alternative. This is contingency planning that answers the "what if" questions. What if you do not pass a certain test? Have another strategy in place until you are tested again. What if you do not lose ten pounds in thirty days? Try different foods and quantities, and extend your time frame to sixty days. Coming to the same negative result by acting with the same strategy means you have to change your strategy. Success includes planning. Have more than one plan in place in case the first one fails. Having more alternatives will have a more positive influence on your desired outcome.

Use symbols to motivate.
Harrison Jeffords

After graduating from the University of Michigan, he became a lawyer and the owner of his father's brickyard. Before leaving home, he discussed with his mother the possibility of never returning, and so he wrote a last will and testament to make certain she would inherit his possessions. Because of the respect he enjoyed from his men, he was promoted rapidly to colonel.

The regimental flag, most often referred to as "the colors," was steadfastly protected because it was an icon in motion, representing the fighting men and boys from the same community. It was the beginning point behind which all soldiers would rally; it was the mid-point around which all forces would collide; it was the end point in which all hopes of victory would endure. The flag was home, consecrated in battle, and it had to be defended to the death.

The colors were so frequently shot to pieces that they had to be replaced. The flag was usually kept clean, and if it ever touched the ground, it was considered bad luck. Jeffords "pledged himself in decisive terms to be its special defender and guardian." In the next few minutes, the Stars and Stripes would also be in serious jeopardy. His vow was about to be tested.

Jeffords was in a hail of gunfire in a wheat field on July 2. His unit was suddenly faced with a charging enemy that easily outnumbered his own. The fighting quickly became hand-to-hand in what was called a "whirlpool of death." In the confusion of the fight, the flag dropped to the ground. Jeffords and two other officers saw the flag and dashed to retrieve it. At the very same time a Confederate grabbed the flag. With both sides screaming and cursing, a battle for the flag itself began. It was a breath-taking moment. The Confederate was killed. Union hearts sank, but only for an instant. Jeffords finally took possession of the flag. After being shot in the leg, one observer remarked later that while Jeffords lay on the ground not willing "to yield the prize, the rebels rushed forward and literally pinned the gallant Jeffords to the earth with bayonets." One bayonet thrust mortally wounded him, but not before the Confederate was shot to death for his deed.

When he was carried from the field, Jeffords's last words reflected the same last thoughts of family when soldiers knew they were near the point of death: "mother, mother, mother!"

Gettysburg Lessons

Use symbols to motivate.

Jeffords shows us that a symbol can elicit powerful emotions, motivating us to act magnificently in a difficult situation. We covet symbols because they inspire. They influence us to think powerful thoughts that lead to powerful actions. For most Americans the Stars and Stripes provides a sense of identity, a feeling of belonging, a motivating expression of that for which we stand, and a stirring reminder of the price our forefathers paid for the freedoms we enjoy. Our national flag goes beyond its intellectual meaning and reaches into our hearts. Therein resides its power, its ability to harness our thoughts and feelings for noble ends. Like nearly everyone on both sides of the fight, Jeffords had a profound emotional investment in his flag, which was an influential symbol that led him to give to his country what Lincoln called "the last full measure of devotion."

Character wins.

George Ward

He came from a family with a proud military tradition. It began with General Artemus Ward who was the first commander of the Continental Army to engage the British at Boston in 1775. Now it was George's turn to carry on a family tradition. He would demonstrate a trait common to many personalities portrayed in this book: character. In a previous battle, a gunshot wound to his left leg resulted in its amputation. A crudely made artificial limb was now a painful companion. A year and a half later, his wound had not healed. Having been granted several leaves of absence from field duty, he nonetheless remained active as a recruiter in his hometown. He was driven to serve his country even though one surgeon wrote, "...the wound being still open is a source of constant irritation in itself, besides acting as a constitutional drain, thus rendering him more liable to disease...."

Medical statements written just six weeks before the great battle declared Ward "unfit for duty." He no longer attempted to heal his wound. Was it because he saw no hope for recovery? Was he resigned to the wound's worst case scenario, death from infection? With words to his wife, Ward was philosophical: "...we must take things as we find them." Having accepted his worsening physical condition, he wrote passionately of his purpose, which was "a deep seated, earnest determination to wipe out the foul blot [of the Confederacy]."

"I have not had my leg off for three days," he wrote a few days before the battle, "neither has it been dressed." After riding on horseback for over one hundred miles, his arrival at the battlefield was a private victory, a self-affirmation, and a dramatic demonstration of personal triumph over a debilitating physical limitation. He was last seen with a "cane in one hand and sword in the other." It was a picture of courage his men would always remember. "The only exact testimony of a man," wrote Thomas Jefferson, "is his actions." Because his courage brought him this far, Ward may well have believed he could accomplish larger victories. He did not get the chance to prove it because this determined man of extraordinary fortitude was killed on the second day in a self-enforced walk toward immortality.

154

Gettysburg Lessons

Character wins.

Why do you help someone in need when there is nothing to gain? Why do you reflect on the ideas and opinions of others that disagree with your own? Why do you work hard when others do not? Why do you stand up for what you believe is right when everyone else considers it inconvenient? Why do you make decisions based on principle when decisions based on public polls are more popular? Why do you take responsibility for your mistakes when you could blame someone else? Why? Because you have character, doing the right thing when doing the wrong thing is so much easier. It gives you the capacity to sacrifice self-interest for the greater good. When you choose to do what is right, you influence others to trust you, or to act in the same way. Moreover, you distinguish yourself with integrity and the common good remains in your protective custody. Character always wins the day, and like Ward, you are the definition of a role model who will help secure the Republic.

Purpose can overcome physical limitations.

Being passionate about something, dedicated totally to a purpose, will make you rise above the ordinary to achieve the extraordinary. Purpose with passion is the ultimate influence. It can overcome physical limitations. At one point in his life, Vietnam veteran Max Cleland could well have written Ward's words himself: "Take things as we find them." Having lost an arm and both legs in a combat environment, Cleland never let his physical condition limit his desire or ability to achieve seemingly unreachable goals. He was elected to represent the state of Georgia in the US Senate in the 1990s. Voters took him as they found him: passionate and purposeful.

Freedom motivates.
Hans Jorgensen

Sophisticated and well-bred, he was once a soldier in the Danish army. Before immigrating to the United States, he was wounded twice while fighting Prussians. Later, his many wounds fighting Rebels would discourage most people from volunteering for combat duty in the Civil War. He became America's ideal immigrant: under no obligation to put himself in danger for his new country, he volunteered, as he put it, "to fight for freedom." It was an ideal whose inspirational content motivated him to rise to the defense of a treasure he believed was worth the price of his own life. "I cheerfully give my life in its defense," he wrote before the battle, and "I would give more if I had it." It was a patriotic sentiment echoed by a Revolutionary War hero, Nathan Hale, who was hung by the British immediately after saying, "I regret that I have but one life to give for my country."

Before arriving at Gettysburg, he participated in over 20 Civil War battles. He could point to his seven scars marking his seven close calls with death. He predicted his own fate before the battle, remarking that he was not going to see the end of the week. "There is no doubt," he wrote in a letter home, "as to the result of this battle. Give my love to all my friends...." He may have agonized with the knowledge that he would not participate in his new nation's birthday, a day he would have been the proudest and the loudest to celebrate. He was killed just 2 days before the 4th of July.

Gettysburg Lessons

Legal immigration inspires.

Legal immigrants are led to America today by the gravitational pull of its freedoms, the same that beckoned Jorgensen. The first immigrants were willing to take great risks, leaving everything behind for the right to live in freedom. Their legacy is uniquely demonstrated by today's self-employed. Like our self-employed founding fathers who came together and started a new nation, self-employed individuals today bring their resources together and start new businesses. New ideas flower in the seedbed of unrestricted freedom. People everywhere know that freedom allows and encourages them to design their own destinies. America takes the Jorgensens of the world into its heart because freedom acts as a magnet to make the most of their energies, talent, and ambitions.

Freedom motivates.

People will fight for freedom because its power is eternal, life-giving, and fragile. These qualities are what set America apart from other nations. Yet some take their freedom for granted, never recognizing their responsibilities as citizens to insure it. With a view that hard work in a free society can advance you spiritually, emotionally, and financially, legal immigrants are welcome reminders of the freedom Americans enjoy everyday.

Many new immigrants teach their children what they can achieve in a free society, and in late spring of every year, Americans witness numerous graduation rituals of first generation Americans who are honored as valedictorians. These achievers influence America by offering two valuable reminders: first, you can succeed, not because you are gifted, but because you can accomplish great things if you are willing to work hard; and second, freedom allows you the opportunities to excel and succeed in a manner and time of your own choosing. A reminder is a second look at what you are fortunate to possess. If you internalize this look and strive to enjoy its benefits, you will likely live a productive life. A legal immigrant can be an inspiring reminder of America's greatness.

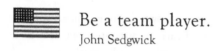

Be a team player.
John Sedgwick

A solitaire player affectionately known as "Uncle John," he was so well respected by his own troops that beginning on the night before the battle, they marched an uncommon thirty-four miles in nineteen hours. It was no easy accomplishment for many soldiers in either army to carry fifty-pound packs for such a distance. During the march, bands were playing and a chorus of some ten thousand voices sang *The Battle Hymn of the Republic.* "Whoever was responsible for it," said one soldier, "it was certainly a happy inspiration and helped the men wonderfully." Grown men felt inspired with the emotional footing of patriotic music and song to quicken their pace toward the days ahead? Sedgwick was the type of leader to provide the right environment for soldiers to do such things.

When Sedgwick arrived at Gettysburg, he was ordered to turn his men over to other units. He simply parceled out groups of men who were needed to support other commanders. Eventually he was a general in command of nothing more than his orderlies.

Sedgwick did not go down in history for any notable defeat of the enemy, it was not his destiny. He did not make any moves to advantage his position above his peers, it was not his inclination. He did not show extraordinary valor, it was not his circumstance. By performing simple administrative duties, he made it possible for his fellow commanders to perform for maximum results. Sedgwick was the ideal team player - unglamorous and unnoticed - and his team won.

Gettysburg Lessons

Be a team player.

When you perform activities that are not part of your job description, as Sedgwick did, it may be to test your ability to perform other tasks. Perhaps you were chosen because your past performance impressed someone with your capabilities. Complete the most seemingly unimportant activity to the best of your ability, and you will influence your employer, your association, or your group toward goals everyone shares. The team succeeds partly because of what you do to influence the outcome.

Expect to do the unexpected.

Sedgwick was called upon to perform tasks that were contrary to what are typically required of generals. At Gettysburg he had to forego what he was trained to do in order to provide another service that benefited the entire team. If you become the owner of your own company, expect to perform every task at some point, including sweeping the floor. Even though you graduate at the top of your class, expect to start at the bottom rung of the organizational ladder.

Create a productive atmosphere.

Many companies provide background music, specific color schemes and lighting in the work environment. Some even include flexible working hours, or provide the option to perform some or all their duties from remote locations. The purpose is to provide a pleasant working atmosphere that influences productivity, increases the overall cohesiveness of the working group, and ultimately amplifies the probability of attaining goals. Sedgwick was not one to discourage his men from having simple pleasures if he thought it would influence their morale and performance.

Lead and succeed at any age.
Tillie Pierce (Gettysburg resident)

The battle of Gettysburg came to her doorstep. Twenty-five years later, she wrote of the terror she felt in the battle that was unfolding right in front of her. Her first reaction was observing the Confederates as "a horrible sight! There they were... Clad almost in rags, covered with dust, riding wildly, pell-mell down the hill toward our home! Shouting, yelling most unearthly, cursing, brandishing their revolvers, and firing right and left."

Tillie Pierce's first experience of the horrors of war came when she saw the effects of a Union soldier blown into the air. As she walked closer to the wounded man, she heard him say, "Oh my God! I didn't read my Bible today. What will my poor wife and children say?" What she saw next was radically foreign to anyone's everyday experiences: the mutilation of a human being. She recounted: "...his eyes are blown out and his whole person seems to be one black mass." Pierce would witness misery everywhere as so many soldiers, suffering horribly, surrounded her. "There were the groaning and crying, the struggling and dying, crowded side by side...." They were "hovering on the verge of Eternity."

For the next three days Pierce carried water to the wounded and dying. Her only restful moments were filled with anxiety and weeping. She observed first hand the grotesque results of battle, witnessing "surgeons sawing and cutting off arms and legs, then again probing and picking bullets from the flesh...." Then, "I noticed a pile of limbs higher than the fence."

Tillie Pierce became a comfort to those who had not seen a youthful female face since leaving home. Her great contribution was acting as a welcome oasis in a field of human misery. The refreshing water she gave, the quiet kindness she expressed, and the simple act of listening were gifts of hope dispensed freely and tenderly to grown men in the last moments of their lives. She took them across an emotional bridge of hope over which few of them could travel alone.

Pierce's recollection, written twenty-five years later, was one of the most poignant accounts of one person's experience of the battle. Moreover, she discovered that we are all heroes under stress: "Nor is it with any desire to be classed among the heroines of that period, that these lines are written; but simply to show what many a patriotic and loyal girl would have done if surrounded by similar circumstances." Twenty-five years earlier, in the most horrific three days of her life, Tillie Pierce was only fifteen-years-old.

Gettysburg Lessons

Lead and succeed at any age.

Success is what you experience from within at any age. Success is leadership of the self: as you put thoughts into motion to improve the lives of others, you are leading yourself from a point of apathy to making a difference. Tillie Pierce clearly had an influence on the lives of those she served; she kept hope alive where there was none. In times of trouble, you can be a comfort to someone in need of a little understanding. You do not need to give advice, or know how to give it. Like Pierce, all you have to do is listen.

Children use their talents under stress.

While the bullets were flying, Pierce employed her previously unknown resources of fortitude and compassion that were so effective with those in her care. Service to others is often touted as the ultimate activity of every great leader, and Tillie Pierce certainly exercised a form of that activity. Do not assume that children cannot demonstrate these qualities simply because they are children. We all possess these qualities simply because we are human.

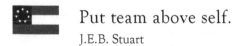

Put team above self.
J.E.B. Stuart

He was a skilled cavalry commander and a dashing glory-hound in search of newspaper headlines. "I'd rather die than be whipped," was his last battle cry. After receiving criticism for his brilliant performance during a surprise Union cavalry charge in a previous battle, Stuart was determined to insure his reputation as an exceptional cavalry officer. His chance came from General Lee who once said that "General Stuart was...always ready for any work and always reliable." Lee gave his subordinate a clear directive to "...move on and feel the right of Ewell's troops, collect information, provisions, etc." But Stuart took a phrase of Lee's order very close to heart, that he was to do "them [the enemy] all the damage you can." This phrase, coupled with a bruised ego, provided the stimulus package Stuart needed to proceed with self-redemption.

Instead of rushing to support another Confederate commander and scouting for enemy positions, Stuart violated his orders and captured well over one hundred wagons of Union supplies, took hundreds of prisoners, and confiscated over four thousand horses and mules. This excess baggage hampered his usual fast pace. Convinced he had the trophies to regain whatever reputation he may have lost, he pushed his men so hard into Pennsylvania that they were too exhausted to fight. Stuart had wasted valuable time, not to mention valuable surveillance activity.

Unable to rely on Stuart for reconnaissance during this critical time, Lee did not know the location of the Union army, and yet was nearing the start of the war's greatest battle. He was now dependent on a single actor-turned-spy for information about the enemy's position and strength. Stuart, whose whereabouts was a mystery for the past eight days, unexpectedly showed up in the middle of the battle announcing his prized gains. Lee sternly rebuked him, declaring that his booty was "...an impediment to me now." Lee concluded after the battle: "The movements of the [Rebel] army preceding the battle of Gettysburg had been much embarrassed by the absence of the cavalry."

The entire incident caused Rebel General Henry Heth to offer his own damaging assessment years later: "The failure to crush the Federal army in Pennsylvania in 1863, in the opinion of almost all the officers of the Army of Northern Virginia, can be expressed in five words--the absence of our cavalry." Stuart temporarily placed his own interests above those of the team. His decision to do so was partly responsible for Lee's eventual defeat.

Gettysburg Lessons

Put team above self.

Stuart lost sight of the importance of teamwork. You have a responsibility to your teammates to put the interests of the team ahead of your own. This is not to say that there is no room for your personal interests or aspirations. In fact, your interests are vital to the team as long as they are used to accomplish the team's objectives - they are the larger influence that can lead you to personal achievement.

Achieving is easier with help.

Past successes like those that gave Stuart a great reputation will not excuse you from making new mistakes. If necessary, seek the guidance of others and leave your ego on the shelf. It may prove difficult, but getting help makes doing things a lot easier. Good leaders must always be good followers.

July 3

The Final Day

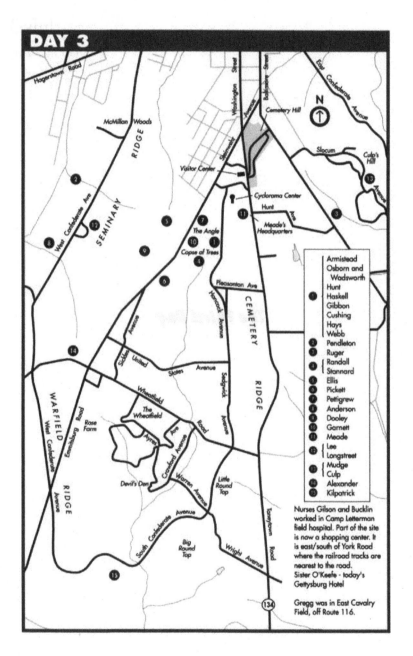

DAY 3

N ↑

McMillan Woods

HOGERSTOWN ROAD

Washington Street

Baltimore Street

East Confederate Avenue

Cemetery Hill

Slocum

Culp's Hill

Avenue

SEMINARY RIDGE

West Confederate Ave

Visitor Center

Steinwehr

The Angle

Copse of Trees

Cyclorama Center

Hunt

Meade's Headquarters

Pleasanton Ave

Hancock Avenue

CEMETERY RIDGE

Sickles Avenue

United

States Avenue

Sedgwick Avenue

WARFIELD RIDGE

West Confederate

Emmitsburg Road

Rose Farm

The Wheatfield

Wheatfield Road

Ayres Ave

Crawford Avenue

Devil's Den

Warren Avenue

Little Round Top

Road

Big Round Top

Wright Avenue

South Confederate Avenue

Taneytown Road

134

	Armistead Osborn and Wadsworth Hunt
❶	Haskell Gibbon Cushing Hays Webb
❷	Pendleton
❸	Ruger Randall Stannard
❹	Ellis
❺	Pickett
❼	Pettigrew
❽	Anderson
❾	Dooley
❿	Garnett
⓫	Meade
⓬	Lee Longstreet
⓭	Mudge Culp
⓮	Alexander
⓯	Kilpatrick

Nurses Gilson and Bucklin worked in Camp Letterman field hospital. Part of the site is now a shopping center. It is east/south of York Road where the railroad tracks are nearest to the road.
Sister O'Keefe - today's Gettysburg Hotel

Gregg was in East Cavalry Field, off Route 116.

Put it in writing.
Thomas Ruger

He graduated near the top of his class at West Point, left the army to study law, and then returned to the military to lead a Wisconsin regiment of volunteers. He was the favorite of a superior officer who once described him in what may strike us today as unusual non-military language: "as modest as a girl but of most thorough and sterling character."

He was a competent leader whose simple error had incredibly tragic consequences. Officers of both armies preferred to issue orders in writing so there would be no mistake as to what action to take. On this occasion Ruger sent one of his staff officers to see Commander Silas Colgrove with directives for his next move. However, this time the instructions were oral.

The events that followed initiated one of the most heartbreaking moments of the battle. What the staff officer said and what Colgrove heard were not synonymous. The original order was to determine the strength of the Confederate forces. What was interpreted was an order to attack. Opposites would attract a catastrophe.

The officer under Colgrove who was subsequently instructed to make the attack was not sure if Colgrove clearly understood what he was ordering, since it was obvious to everyone hearing the order that its fulfillment would put two regiments in extreme jeopardy. Colgrove remembered: "The enemy's advantages were such that a line of [our] skirmishers would be cut down before they could fairly gain the open ground that intervened. The only possible chance I had to advance was to carry [the Confederate] position by storming it." In other words, fake out your opponent by doing something totally unexpected, if not incredibly stupid, and hope you will win the day.

The order was carried out, but not before the attacking officer was heard to say, "...it is murder, but it's the order." The moments that followed witnessed incredible valor and an unimaginable waste of human life. Ruger suggested later that there was a misunderstanding. His only

167

comment about what happened fell far short of what could have been said: "The regiments selected...moved forward gallantly...." In a few horrifying minutes, nearly three hundred soldiers lay dead or wounded, all because someone neglected to communicate with a piece of paper.

Gettysburg Lessons

Put it in writing.

Communication can be tricky. That is why there are pens, paper, word processors, barrels of ink, and electronic messages to scroll simple, declarative sentences such as, "Determine your competitor's strengths before you make a move." Do not assume that a subordinate understands a simple oral instruction, or that you understand a superior's oral directive. Written communications will influence success, or failure. It is not suggested that every communication be in writing, only those that have an important impact on how your objectives are reached.

To put something in writing is generally meant to avoid any misunderstanding. Not wanting King George III to misunderstand, Thomas Jefferson put the sentiments of an infant nation in writing with the Declaration of Independence; not wanting the country to misunderstand the purpose of the Civil War, Abraham Lincoln put his thoughts in writing with the Gettysburg Address; not wanting customers to misunderstand a transaction, businesses put their sales agreements in a written receipt.

If you have any doubt about what someone said, write it down. The written word is a visual, tangible mechanism to clarify, qualify, and quantify. To be successful, write down your goals so you can see them often, or else they are only wishes with no visual clarity to trigger the passion needed for their accomplishment.

Question what you hear.
Charles Mudge

He refused to conform to Harvard's strict rules of demeanor and academic performance. Prior to graduation his father received a letter from Harvard's president suggesting that his son would not be awarded his degree until he showed more maturity. "His work [is] imperfectly performed," complained school officials, "and he has persisted in disregarding the rules of order in the college." In other words, he is a continuous frat-boy nuisance, and Harvard's patience has been exhausted.

When the war began, "Charley" Mudge wrote to his father that he wanted "to fight, and when I say fight I mean win or die." With apparent resignation to a son's fate, the father wrote back to Harvard's president asking that his son's degree be conferred, explaining "...my son may never return...the reasons will doubtless be sufficiently apparent to the Faculty." Young Mudge received his degree just days before he left Boston for Virginia.

He did what he could to prepare for the hardships ahead. He would sleep on bare ground when it was not necessary. It was a self-imposed, basic training exercise. During his enlistment he carried a prayer book, and every Sunday morning he would lead his men in a prayer service. "You have no idea," he wrote his father, "what comfort I have had from perfect faith in God..."

On the morning of July 3, history was contriving to force Mudge into a futile attack on a very secure enemy position. An eager and overly aggressive superior thought there was no other way to gain ground than to charge the enemy, hoping they would be frightened enough to abandon their location. Intuitively, Mudge knew it was a death sentence. Wanting to be certain he was hearing the correct orders, he asked, "Are you sure that is the order?" A simple "yes" was the reply. Mudge was faced with a soldier's unimaginable choice: he could obey a military order that meant certain death, or disobey it and face certain court-martial and personal disgrace. Soon after uttering the words, "Well, it is murder, but it is the order," this twenty-four-year-old officer was killed.

We will never know what he was thinking during his last moments. We can only assume that Mudge, though questioning the correctness of the order, felt some greater good would come from such a fruitless and wasteful attack. Having been slightly wounded in two previous battles, he knew the moment had come when he would have to give his life for his country. He could not have imagined *how*.

Gettysburg Lessons

Question what you hear.

Mudge knew instinctually that a superior's decision would kill him. Perhaps other than in a military situation, if you believe a superior's decision will influence you adversely, you have the right and the responsibility to question the reasons behind the decision. If the decision remains unchanged, you can decide not to implement it and accept the consequences. Rarely does a superior earn blind obedience.

Encourage input from subordinates.

As a superior you have a leader's responsibility to enforce your expectations fairly and without undue hardship. You also have an incentive to encourage positive input. This is where Mudge's superiors failed. Soliciting feedback from your subordinates - allowing yourself to be influenced - will keep you moving toward your goals and avoiding pitfalls. It is more profitable to listen than to speak, to be a leader who is willing to follow good advice.

Try.

Francis Randall

He was related to the Revolutionary War soldier and legend, Ethan Allen, of Vermont's Green Mountain Boys. At Gettysburg two very special soldiers were related to Randall: his two sons. One was a junior officer and the other a twelve-year-old drummer boy. One can only imagine the anguish suffered by a wife and mother at home.

Randall had recently recruited a new group of soldiers whose commitment to service was only ninety days. Their jobs were menial: guard duty on railroads, or building fortifications and roads. They had no battle experience, and within days they would be discharged. They thought the war was an unpleasant drudgery that would soon be over. They did not know they were about to be involved in the war's greatest battle on the last day of fighting.

When asked in a stressful moment if his men could fight, Randall responded, "...my regiment being a new organization has seen but little fighting, but I have unbounded confidence in them." Yet one incident described later by a private in Randall's regiment would clarify his perception of men not accustomed to battle. He wrote: "...a whole regiment (what was left of it) came running...to escape the deadly shower of shot and shell that hailed down among them. They were simply frightened and were seeking cover against danger..." Randall could have arrested these men for desertion, but instead he

> ...placed himself in front of these boys...and tried to shame them and restore confidence by referring to his boys of the 13th, saying to them... "See these boys, they don't run and they were never in a battle; you ought to be ashamed to run because a few shells are being fired over this way, better hasten back to your position..." The officers of that regiment, with Colonel Randall's assistance, induced them to return to their position and back they went up the hill in good order no doubt feeling ashamed for their momentary undue weakness and folly.

Randall and his men later faced an opponent who had captured cannons he was asked to retake. Due to the inexperience of his soldiers, Randall harbored some doubt as to whether he could get the job done. "I told him [General Hancock] I thought I could, and that I was willing to try." After giving the order, "my men sprang forward with the bayonet with so much precipitancy that they [the Rebels] appeared to be taken wholly by surprise...surrendering..." With some knee-bruising along the way, Randall succeeded in his attempt, but not before his officer-son endured the scare of his life. Prior to his father retrieving the cannons that were captured earlier, his son witnessed his father and horse fall to the ground. Assuming the worst he rushed to his father and saw that only the horse had been shot.

General Hancock observed the results of Randall's men and shouted: "That was well done! Give me Vermonters for a charge."

What Randall accomplished next was what career officers dream about, that is, having a substantial impact on the course of a major fight. Randall led his men on a flanking attack hitting the Confederates from the side as they were moving forward. His men so crippled the Confederates during Pickett's Charge that he had to order his men to cease-fire. Fortunately for Mrs. Randall, she was able to see her husband and sons again.

Gettysburg Lessons

Try.

If you do not try at the first opportunity to do anything, you may never get another chance. Or, if you simply do not try, you will never know if you would have succeeded. Lack of experience usually holds people back from acting. But with no experience, Randall tried and succeeded. Based on successes in your past, regardless of how small, your self-confidence will influence you to try possibilities never before considered. The first step in self-confidence is to accept your past achievements as real and indisputable. Or, as Yoda in *Star Wars* would say, "Do or not do. There is no try."

Seize opportunity quickly.

George Stannard

He joined his state's militia when he was only sixteen. Highly regarded by those who knew him, he was at different times a farmer, teacher, clerk and foundry operator. Stannard eventually became the leader of his own militia unit and the first person in Vermont to volunteer for service in the Union army.

On the third day at Cemetery Ridge, the end-point of the rebel attack, General Doubleday witnessed Stannard in action and screamed, "Glory to God! Glory to God! Look at those Vermonters go...!"

During Pickett's Charge the Confederates were coming directly toward the Vermonters, but they soon veered off to the left. Stannard knew an opportunity was presenting itself. If he delayed, his target of opportunity would pass. If he acted immediately, the Confederates would be within the right range of fire and at the right angle of movement. Marching his men out, Stannard ordered a ninety-degree turn and inflicted a murderous fire that crippled the South's final attempt to break through the Union line. He later observed with pride that the enemy "did not thus escape the warm reception prepared for them by the Vermonters ...although it was for most of them their first battle."

His men were inexperienced, untested, and derided by veterans who knew they were "nine-monthers," citizen-soldiers who were headed for home after only nine months of service. Because of his ability to lead and his decisiveness and willingness to seize an opportunity quickly, Stannard dealt a severe blow to the opposition from which there was no recovery.

Not within many battles, but within a few minutes, Stannard and his men won glory that only hardened veterans could imagine for themselves. With exaggerated praise, Abner Doubleday said they "performed perhaps the most brilliant feat during the war. They broke the desperate charge of Pickett, saved the day and with it, the whole North from invasion and devastation." Within six weeks, by stark contrast, Stannard's new veterans were back to the natural rhythms and rigors of farming.

Gettysburg Lessons

Seize opportunity quickly.

In the game of life, your ever-present opponents are the calendar and the clock. Hesitate while the window of opportunity is open and you risk losing, or coming in second. Be a Stannard and follow the influences provided by your competitor's weaknesses. They will lead you to make better informed and counter-offensive decisions.

What counts is what you do today.

Continually remind yourself: what really counts is not what I will do someday (this is a self-inflicted set-up to do nothing), but what I will do today to achieve my objectives. Plan and execute. Planning is the influence that leads to your objectives.

Limited opportunity demands decisions.

In a pressure situation where opportunity is severely limited, as it was for Stannard, make decisions early to control the outcome. And trust your instincts - your gut influences - to make those decisions quickly.

A leader is a follower.

George Meade

As the ideal commander of all Union forces at Gettysburg, Major General George Gordon Meade had almost perfect pitch for interpreting the language of the battlefield. By consulting continually with subordinates, he adapted quickly to changing conditions. To make informed and sensible decisions, he assigned an aide to each of his commanders whose duty was to report the latest positions and combat status of his troops. Knowing practically every detail allowed him to plan for nearly every contingency in a crisis-management mode. In short, Meade was the master manager of timely information that allowed him to win his greatest victory and a permanent residence in posterity.

It was not until the early hours of June 28, just three days before the battle, that Meade was put in charge of an eighty-five-thousand-man army. The effect on him was evident in a letter to his wife written two days later: "I continue well, but much oppressed with a sense of responsibility.... Of course, in time I will become accustomed to this." It was another way of saying, "I'm under a lot of pressure, but I'll handle it." After the battle one of his generals remarked that Meade's "moral character was a tower of strength and gave hope to the hearts of those who...believed in the success of a just cause."

Although Union forces eventually won the battle, enough of Meade's commanders were wounded, his forces battered, disorganized, and too exhausted to make a fast, follow-up crushing blow of Lee's army to end the war. Even when Meade sought an opportunity to pursue Lee, he clearly understood the limitations of human endurance. Since it was late in the day, even the timing was wrong. Which may be why Meade's decision *not* to act deserves special credit. He was wise not to take the offensive and initiate the Union version of Lee's disastrous charge across the same field, subject to the same hazardous conditions with nearly ten thousand Rebels in waiting and eager for a fight. History had crafted his last hours of the battle to be a defensive holding action.

For his achievement Meade was cited and later promoted for bringing "his forces into action at the right time and place, which no commander of the Army of the Potomac had done before." He accomplished his sole objective, "to maneuver and fight in such a manner as to cover the capital and also Baltimore." Meade was not ordered to do anything more. Even when he wanted to go beyond his orders - to crush Lee once and for all, the handicapped condition of his key commanders and troops held him back. What he could not foresee was disapproval for not doing more than was ordered.

Two weeks later president Lincoln wrote a letter to Meade criticizing him for not pursuing Lee and ending the war. In hindsight, Lincoln changed Meade's objective two weeks *after* the battle was already won. On reflection a frustrated president knew better not to send the letter, but its substance was communicated to Meade who then offered to resign. The president refused him, knowing his censure of Meade was a mistake; Lincoln did not fully appreciate Meade's condition on the ground.

The short-term goal in warfare is winning a battle so that the long-term objective of ending a war is accomplished. Not ending the war at Gettysburg was ultimately no one's fault. Lincoln can be criticized rightfully for not communicating to Meade his vision of achieving the long-term goal, but it strains credulity to deny Meade's near-impossible conditions that prevented him from accomplishing an army's ultimate purpose.

Gettysburg Lessons

A leader is a follower.

Great leaders are also great followers. Meade was working with *mandatory* influences: military orders. He obeyed them so well that he won the greatest battle of the Civil War, earned immediate praise from his superiors in Washington, and was awarded a permanent promotion. All leaders have an idea to follow, be it mandatory or discretionary.

Have a little more than enough.

Just as Meade could not win a war without an inventory of fresh troops and food, you cannot buy a home with too little money, or run a business with too little capital. You cannot achieve an "A" in a course of study if you do not use every available and honorable means to make the grade. You cannot be a successful parent if you do not spend extra time with your children. There are times when leading requires a little more effort than you are prepared to give.

A competitor's mistakes can help you.

When your opponents expose their moves, as Lee did to Meade during the last day, they can make costly mistakes. They will influence you to predict future actions, prepare for them, and make counter moves that give you a clear advantage.

Strong morals allow you to endure.

Strong moral character, as exemplified by Meade, influences you and others to endure pressure and remain focused on your objectives.

Teamwork achieves goals.

Meade was in constant touch with his subordinates and called meetings with his commanders to seek their advice. He provided a stimulus-response environment to determine his next move. It was management of short-term objectives at its best. To listen is to influence others to contribute their ideas. Meade was able to get valuable input and support in a teamwork effort to make the right decisions. End result: Meade won.

Have a vision.
Robert E. Lee

His father, "Light Horse Harry" Lee, was a Revolutionary War hero who abandoned his wife and family to a life of poverty. Robert graduated second in his class at West Point and became an army engineer. He later assumed the role of superintendent of his alma mater where he gave one of his best advisories: "Young men must not expect to escape contact with evil, but must learn not to be contaminated by it." While leading West Point, he maintained a friendship with a previous superintendent, Jefferson Davis. When Davis became the president of the Confederacy, he asked Lee to be his chief military adviser and then commander of what was becoming the Army of Northern Virginia.

Lee was a kind man with a great sense of fairness. He never allowed himself to rebuke a subordinate regardless of rank. A private was once ushered into his tent for a rule infraction. Lee tried to calm the trembling youth by stating, "You've nothing to fear, son, you'll get equal justice here." The young man's response was unforgettable: "Sir, that's what I'm afraid of!"

His profound religious convictions, trusting God completely to determine all outcomes, was sometimes guilt-ridden. He assumed that whenever he was despondent about doing his duty so far away from his sickly wife, it was "a just punishment for my sins."

He took calculated risks to defeat an adversary who had greater advantages in men, guns and supplies. Yet he was unimpressed with his own triumphs, and saw the need to develop a convincing strategy for final victory. But time was running out. His vision of an independent South could not bargain with the damnable particulars of his urgent circumstances: he was up against increasing shortages in manpower, transportation, food, not to mention plummeting civilian support, rising desertion rates, unfilled officer vacancies, and a deep personal depression over the very recent loss of his finest commander, "Stonewall" Jackson. Additionally, poor eyesight, angina, and exhaustion added to the frustration of his efforts.

To compound his difficulties, a subordinate commander was denied assistance from his superior, A.P. Hill, to seize an opportunity that may have won the battle in its first hours. Another officer, a commander of cavalry, ignored Lee's order to be the eyes and ears of his army when they were most needed. Such behaviors only served to give Union forces the time and ground needed to fend off a strong adversary. History had planned too many surprises for Lee.

Lee wanted Gettysburg to be the final blow to the North, reasoning that victory on northern soil would guarantee independence for the South. His unconventional tactics and bold offensive maneuvers led many to believe he could not lose a war he once called "this protracted and sanguinary conflict." Trusting God, Lee ignored tested commander Longstreet's advice not to order an attack through an open field that dangerously exposed his army. Even his battle planners did not take into account the mundane and inconvenient detail of post-and-rail fences that would impede the final attack. Pickett's Charge was a misstep in the extreme. Lee's best-laid plan was no longer visionary: he could not see that he and history were on a collision course.

Five weeks after the battle, a despondent and sickly Lee waxed philosophical about his defeat at Gettysburg: "We must expect reverses, even defeats. They are sent to teach us wisdom and prudence, to call forth greater energies, and to prevent our falling into greater disasters." Characteristically, Lee framed the loss in religious sentiments reminiscent of similar words he used years before when he was far away from his wife: "Soldiers! We have sinned against Almighty God. We have forgotten His signal mercies, and have cultivated a revengeful, haughty, and boastful spirit." Seeing himself, in effect, as God's failed agent at a crucial moment in history, Lee offered to resign. But it was an offer, especially from an icon, that his president was forced to reject.

The great paradox of this remarkable warrior is that he was so dependent on God's will for final results. If God was the master manipulator, Lee was the prayerful pawn.

Gettysburg Lessons

Have a vision.

Lee was an effective leader because he had a vision: he was motivated by a quest for an independent nation. Vision was the beacon that guided him to Gettysburg. By its powerful influence, vision is the energizing force that leads you to act with confidence and to act boldly and decisively. What you have planned for yourself in five or ten years is the vision that influences you to act now.

Check and recheck.

Be absolutely clear about what you expect from others. Do not allow talented subordinates so much discretion that you neglect to monitor their plans and execution, as Lee did with Longstreet on the third day. You must act as a check-and-balance to provide guidance. An understanding of how you think influences the results you expect from their own decision-making. A leader's monitoring leads the group in the desired direction. When acting alone, check and recheck your information. Seek an outside yet reliable second opinion. Examine the pros and cons in writing before making a decision that can have far-reaching consequences.

Take the blame.

One sure sign of being a great leader is taking ultimate responsibility for your own mistakes. When Lee knew that he was defeated, he did not blame anyone but himself. "It is my fault," he said to his troops after the battle, "it is all my fault."

You can be a great leader.

Have a goal and design a plan to achieve it. Anticipate obstacles even when some appear to be mundane. Belief in achieving your goal and sticking to your design will influence others to follow you.

Wishful thinking fails.

Porter Alexander

In charge of bombing the Federal forces on the third day, this twenty-seven-year-old was placed in a very awkward command position. General Longstreet gave him a most unusual written message suggesting that Alexander, an artillery commander and a subordinate, should decide *if* and *when* a major infantry attack ought to begin. In the protocol of command, it was not his decision to make, it was Longstreet's. Predictably, Alexander was dumbfounded.

With an exchange of messages between them, Alexander, like so many other Southern commanders, suffered from Lee-Can't-Fail Syndrome. With so much confidence in Lee's decision to win with a grand assault on the Union line, he had no doubts that the attack would succeed, no matter what the opposition had in store. This was a chunk of wishful thinking that defied the unpleasant certainties of battle. Faced with the prospect that he would have to give the order for Pickett to advance, reality hit him squarely in the solar plexus. With the heavy smoke of battle blurring his vision to judge fairly the effects of his own artillery bombardment, preparatory to an infantry assault, he could not determine the effectiveness of his own cannon fire. Feeling uncomfortable in an unusual exchange with a commanding officer, Alexander was diplomatic in avoiding a responsibility that was not his, and awaited further orders.

Gettysburg Lessons

Wishing thinking fails.

Failure is an offspring of delusion. Success is a product of good judgment. If belief in your success is like Alexander's, based on wishful thinking, you will fail. Perform a due diligence, that is, give an opportunity its due by examining its potential with diligence. This will place you in an ideal position to judge the merits of an opportunity. The facts will influence you to make a good decision.

You cannot solve every problem.
James Longstreet

Enjoying physical training over intellectual challenges and schoolboy pranks over blind obedience, he graduated near the bottom of his class at West Point. He never looked back as he distinguished himself as a shrewd tactician in the first battles of the war. He soon caught General Lee's attention and became second in command of his Army of Northern Virginia.

As a poker player he chose to calculate his next move to increase the odds in his favor rather than depend on pure luck. As much as he respected the offensive tactics of his commander, Longstreet preferred to take defensive positions and plan carefully.

He was a bit of an oddity: he rarely became animated about anything, fathered ten children but never mentioned his wife in his memoirs, took a short nap just before the most intense moments at Gettysburg, and incensed the South after the war by abandoning his prior loyalty to "The Lost Cause" - an independent South.

A valued and tested commander loyal to General Lee, Longstreet disagreed with his superior on what he regarded as an impossible attack plan on the third day, or what became known as Pickett's Charge. Anticipating disaster he urged Lee, almost to the point of insubordination, to consider an alternative attack proposal. Lee listened to his "Old War Horse," but his plan of action had already been decided in consultation with several generals and his aides. As an obedient officer Longstreet gave the nod to Pickett for the attack to begin, but not before he made an unsuccessful attempt to subcontract the attack decision to his artillery commander instead, thereby passing off responsibility to a subordinate and exposing inner doubts that reflected an internal wrestling match. This was one poker hand he did not want to play. With disaster just minutes away, and with the greatest reluctance, he had to convert the impossible into the inescapable.

Longstreet was fated to make the most agonizing decisions of any commander during the battle. Lee's plan called for an attack sequel. At least another ten thousand men were ready and standing by to exploit any advantage, or give needed support. But Longstreet's battlefield credentials told him Lee's plan spelled disaster. Just moments before the charge, Longstreet told his chief artillerist, Porter Alexander: "I do not want to make this attack...I don't see how it can succeed." To reveal his state of mind, he uttered to General Pickett: "...I am being crucified at the thought of the sacrifice of life which this attack will make." The remark made Pickett observe later that Longstreet had given the go-ahead for the battle to begin "against his own convictions, ~ given in anguish and with reluctance." Longstreet was engaged in a poignant internal struggle: he was torn between obeying his orders and exercising his own good judgment. He advanced halfway by ordering Lee's initial attack but not his follow-up plan. Longstreet was looking down the double barrels of an order that held him hostage in the crucible of the moment.

While his soldiers were being slaughtered, support troops watched in silent horror. It never crossed the minds of anyone on the field that day that Longstreet alone was struggling with decisions he could not justify and expectations he could not satisfy. He later lamented, "...never was I so depressed as upon that day." His mental anguish, blurring the clarity needed of a commander to make wise decisions, could well have contributed to a Rebel casualty toll of more than six thousand men in less than an hour. Conversely, it may have prevented a greater number of casualties so that Lee's army could fight another day. With little hope going in, and virtually none coming out, Longstreet's dilemma crafted the coffin for Southern independence.

Gettysburg Lessons

Some situations are no-wins.

Take the initiative. Tactfully suggest alternative actions that can prevent what appears to be a wrong decision by your superiors. Lead by the influence of powerful ideas. Just as your past experiences may indicate that a superior's decision will do more harm than good, take action to the extent to which you are obligated, even if your recommendations to do otherwise go unheeded as they did for

Longstreet. The outcome is not your responsibility. More importantly, your conscience is clear.

Your obligation to implement a poor decision will have you struggling between what your own experience tells you to do and what you are told to do. Therein resides your own Longstreet dilemma. If you cannot change the outcome and instead attempt to put it off, you have made a decision to do nothing, which can prove to be a poor decision. You remain helpless and anxious with no solution in sight that will better your situation, define your direction, or give you hope all the while awaiting the inevitable. Attempts to control your circumstances are preempted when indecisiveness takes control. No matter who you are, there will be a time when you will find yourself, like Longstreet, in a no-win situation.

You cannot solve every problem.

Longstreet's dilemma demonstrates that he was all too human. He had to come to terms with deeply troubling decisions he was forced to execute, none of which he created and whose consequences were out of his control. When a helpless physician presents a terminally-ill patient with choices, they all lead inevitably to the patient's demise. One can feel Longstreet's gut-wrenching anxiety in his own words: "I felt that my men were to be sacrificed and that I should have to order them to make a hopeless charge."

Have a deadline.

On the second day of the battle Longstreet was ordered by Lee to make his attack at 10 a.m. Due to a multitude of factors, Longstreet's attack began hours later. Had he met the deadline, Longstreet may have been more successful. A deadline forces you to concentrate your energies within a specific time-frame so you know when the job has to be done. It is a target to aim at, an influence that forces careful planning, a commitment to action, and generates enthusiasm to achieve your objectives on time.

Surrender control, or take control.

George Pickett

He was an incurable romantic. He was writing a love letter to his fiancé just minutes before the famous charge that immortalized his name. Since he anticipated the coming charge as a moment of greatness for himself, he was now in the grips of a dangerous fantasy. He felt a bit giddy, but in no way did he imagine that he would be trapped in the middle of one of American history's most dramatic turning points. Nothing distracted him from his desire for fame, not even comments about his perfumed hair whose scent lingered long enough to raise a few eyebrows. "As he passed me, he rode gracefully," wrote his commander James Longstreet, "with his jaunty cap racked well over his right ear and his long auburn locks, nicely dressed, hanging almost to his shoulders. He seemed a holiday soldier."

He was the son of a wealthy Virginia plantation owner, studied law, and was accepted to West Point. Pickett did not distinguish himself at the military school - he graduated last in his class. Twice widowed he began courting young LaSalle Corbell, sometimes leaving his division without permission to see her. They married after the battle and later had two children.

Pickett hung twenty-two Union soldiers who were once Confederates, subsequently fleeing with his family to Canada to avoid being tried for war crimes. Three years after the war he was granted a full pardon under President Andrew Johnson's general amnesty. The Picketts moved back to Virginia, and George was able to make a respectable living in the insurance business until he died at the age of fifty.

Before Gettysburg, Pickett had never led a full division into battle. Anxious to win accolades for himself, Pickett's Charge was planned to scare and confuse the enemy enough so that support units could follow up and quickly move in and do their destruction. It began as what many Union veterans said later was a grand parade that turned into an all-too-easy shooting gallery, resulting in Pickett's forces being massacred under heavy fire. As his surviving men limped back from the disaster, he sent one of his aides to his commander, General Longstreet, pleading for immediate support. The aide was instructed to tell Pickett that the support he expected was not coming, that the battle was lost. In modern colloquial terms, Pickett was being thrown under the bus.

When the charge was over, Lee approached Pickett to ask the whereabouts of his division. Pickett's response sounded the agony of a broken man: "General Lee, I have no division now." Profoundly distraught by the results of the battle, this romantic-turned-realist wrote to his future wife 3 days later:

> I can't write you a love-letter to-day, my Sallie, for with my great love for you and my gratitude to God for sparing my life to devote to you, comes the over-powering thought of those whose lives were sacrificed, of the broken-hearted widows and mothers and orphans. The moans of my wounded boys, the sight of the dead, upturned faces, flood my soul with grief and here am I whom they trusted, whom they followed, leaving them on that field of carnage...

George Pickett was the only Rebel general at Gettysburg who never received praise or mention from Lee, either in his official reports or in post-war reminiscences. Pickett never forgave Lee for what happened at Gettysburg. Some years later and immediately after an uneasy visit with Lee, Pickett complained to an old friend, "That old man had my division slaughtered at Gettysburg." After a brief silence the friend replied, "Well, it made you immortal."

Gettysburg Lessons

Surrender control, or take control.

No matter how successful you want to be, if you are not in control of your own destiny, your hopes and dreams can be frustrated at any time on someone else's whim. It can come in the form of being fired from an ideal job, being passed over for a well-earned promotion, or, in the case of Pickett, not receiving the support you expect. It is the price you pay for allowing others to control your life, with the exception of being a soldier where relinquishing control is required in order to be a part of an effective fighting team.

Ask for help, but plan for none.

When Pickett saw that his troops needed support at the most crucial point of the charge, he was not so stubborn or delusional to believe that he could do it alone. He asked for reinforcements from his superior and friend, General Longstreet, only to be told that support was not coming. It was a cruel surprise for Pickett, and it stands as an all-too-real possibility in any endeavor.

Before you begin any organized, long-term activity, seek agreement with your plan from your superior. Plan and act as if you expect no support. In fact, your expectations could be halted or undermined by superiors. Even without agreement beforehand, assume you must succeed by the influence that comes from taking stock of your own talents, and then viewing any support from above as a bonus.

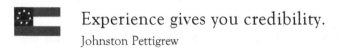

Experience gives you credibility.

Johnston Pettigrew

He was a talented pianist, boxer, fencer, and mathematician. With the highest grade-point average at the University of North Carolina, the president of the United States appointed him as a college professor of astronomy at the age of nineteen. He learned six languages while studying in Europe, staying long enough to write an authoritative four hundred-and-thirty-page book on Spain. He later returned home as a Renaissance man to practice law.

He was a Greek philosopher's ideal man: of sound mind and body, one should experience the rigors of being a soldier. There was talk among influential friends that a position as Chief Justice was in his future, perhaps even the presidency. Pettigrew's talents were soon recognized, and he was promoted through the ranks from private to general, but not before sustaining serious wounds in battle. Pettigrew was the first Rebel officer to spot enemy movements at Gettysburg.

Few officers on the field at Gettysburg commanded more respect from their troops than Pettigrew. One of his officers wanted "no higher honor than to have been a member of his command." Others remarked that he was "the idol of his men..." with "a courage which nothing could daunt." But he was never cavalier about fighting. Instead, he was observant and prudent to a fault, relaying accurate information to his superiors so as not to instigate a battle at the wrong time.

Perhaps due to his lack of hardened battle experience, two superior commanders did not take him seriously when he reported that the enemy was close at hand. Good eyesight, not his military training, was all that was necessary. Still, his commanders precipitated their own misfortunes: Hill was immobilized and Heth had his troops cut to pieces in the battle's initial fight. Both chose to hear Pettigrew's warning through the filter of their own impulses.

The day's fighting left Pettigrew with a casualty rate in excess of forty percent. After a day's recuperation with his battered and demoralized troops, he would understand what it meant to be in the wrong place at the wrong time. By pure coincidence, his men were camped where the battle was going to begin the next day. He ended up marching into American military history's most famous charge.

After having his horse shot from under him during the final minutes of the battle, he proceeded on foot making every attempt to keep his North Carolinians moving forward. A shell fragment shattered his left hand, but the ghastly wound did not stop him. To no one's surprise, with some six thousand Rebel casualties on the field at the battle's end, he was one of the last to leave. Though he led his men well, one of his regiments went in with six hundred men and came out with only a hundred. Pettigrew would not honor the next day as his nation's birthday, nor would he celebrate his own - the 4th of July.

Gettysburg Lessons

Experience gives you credibility.

Pettigrew lacked credibility, not leadership, with his superiors because he had less command experience. You become an asset to others when you have proven yourself repeatedly as someone who knows what you are doing. To the contrary, your inexperience can influence others to take actions you find objectionable.

Courage is a substitute for experience.

Pettigrew stuck it out to the end, not abandoning his mission or his men. Demonstrating courage in the face of adversity is the best influence; it inspires others to act accordingly. It also gives you the fortitude to handle unknowns. Scott Beamer had no experience with terrorism before 9/11, but his courage on Flight 93 over Pennsylvania influenced a result praised by most Americans.

Elevate wisdom above age.

Wisdom comes with learning experiences. If you have learned from your experiences, your age is irrelevant. Experiences, and plenty of them, propel you from being boring to being appealing, and being appealing presents more opportunities to influence.

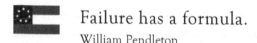

Failure has a formula.

William Pendleton

In the early 1830s he was an artillerist, a college professor, and an Episcopal priest. Some members of his congregation were Southern militia who convinced him to be their instructor in the art of killing by cannon. It is richly ironic that he went from the pulpit to the gun pit after considering how he was going to reconcile his religious life with a military one. How he did it proved puzzling if not irrational, particularly when his four cannons were named after the New Testament writers: John, Matthew, Luke and Mark.

In the tradition of bishops of the Middle Ages, he never missed the chance to sermonize the troops. Before one battle, it was said that he directed his guns at the enemy, raised a hand and shouted, "May the Lord have mercy on their poor souls." As he quickly brought down his hand, he yelled, "Fire!"

On the third day, contrary to what was expected of an experienced cannoneer, he had no idea of the amount of ammunition he had available for his artillery units, nor did he take responsibility or initiative for providing adequate supplies. Moreover, he ordered artillery wagons to the rear without informing anyone, especially his commander General Lee, making the search for ammunition a desperate activity at the worst possible moment. He did not supervise or double-check the placement of cannons as part of Lee's coordinated plan to support the infantry on the first day. Later, Pendleton deluded himself by writing an inaccurate assessment of what really happened, not to mention that the Union army had won the battle: "But if this and other causes prevented our sweeping the enemy from his position, he was so crippled as to be incapable of any formidable movement."

Because he loved to preach, one might conclude that he had no enthusiasm for battle. Because of his ineptitude at Gettysburg, the Confederate infantry was not given proper artillery support on the first or third days. As a result, they suffered a devastating loss due, in part, to "Parson Pendleton."

Gettysburg Lessons

Failure has a formula.

If you have no desire to do your work, do not believe in the purpose of your work, or, in the case of Pendleton, are not fulfilling even the basic requirements of your work, you are failing. You are achieving negative results by the powerful influence of your negative thoughts.

Surround yourself with competence.

If you associate with an individual who is unsuited to an assigned task, as Lee did with Pendleton, you will experience problems. As a leader, one of your obligations is to help those who need your help, and the competent individuals will succeed on their own. It is your obligation to influence your company, organization, group, or family to succeed. Therefore, be cautious to promote anyone who will likely demonstrate incompetence in a new position. Otherwise, returning that person to his or her previous level of responsibility will prove difficult.

Self-control allows you to concentrate.
Thomas Osborn and Craig Wadsworth

Major Thomas Osborn commanded a Union artillery unit that was taking direct hits from Rebel cannons immediately prior to Lee's grandest assault. His "guns were hit and knocked off their carriages," he later remarked, adding that "ammunition chests were blown up and horses were going down by the half dozen." Major Osborn best describes the ideal personal disposition in such a stressful situation:

> During such time, the force of will which an officer must bring to bear upon himself in order not only to control his men but also to govern himself, is wonderful. He must by sheer force of will shut up every impulse of his nature, except that of controlling the officers and men subject to his command. He must discard all care of his personal safety and even his own life. The difficult person to control is always himself.

With a hint of self-deprecation to illustrate this self-control, Osborn related an incident when he met with one of General Meade's aids, Captain Wadsworth, in a "hailstorm of flying lead." Both were sitting on their horses.

> While we were talking, a percussion shell struck the ground directly under the horses and exploded. The momentum of the shell carried the fragments along so that neither horse was struck nor did either horse move. When the shell exploded, I was in complete control of my nerves and did not move a muscle of my body or my face. Neither did Wadsworth, but I dropped my eyes to the ground where the shell exploded, and Wadsworth did not. I never quite forgave myself for looking down to the ground when that shell exploded under us. I do not believe that there was a man in the entire army, save Captain Wadsworth, who could have a ten pound shell explode under him without looking where it struck.

Osborn would have us believe that he was not as self-controlled as Wadsworth. To the contrary, God saw fit to make them a pair of stone walls.

In the crucible of the moment, Osborn's imagination went into high gear. Under so much enemy cannon fire, he suggested to General Hunt that the artillery cease firing along the entire Union line. The intent was two-fold: first, to save ammunition for a possible Confederate infantry charge, and second, to give the Rebels the impression that the Union had been defeated in the cannonade. Lee's officers would be influenced to press his plan for a great assault that would deliver the final blow to the Union. Osborn's idea was quickly executed; the trap was set. Lee ordered his men into an open field where they ultimately received some of the most destructive cannon fire of the entire war.

Gettysburg Lessons

Self-control allows you to concentrate.
The exploding shells around you are life's daily distractions, and self-control will help ensure that you remain focused on what you have to do. Without it you cannot be a positive influence.

Be aggressive.
Be an Osborn: speak up! The influence of a simple suggestion may save a relationship, a company, a life, or a country.

Think out of the box.
You can originate great ideas in an environment of tension and pressure. Osborn's crafty suggestion at one of the most dangerous points in the battle helped win the day. His textbook training did not include how to employ clever deception, a creative use of the imagination in one of his most stressful moments. It was a classic example of thinking out of the box, not following by-the-book procedures at a critical time. The most influential ideas can originate from anyone on your team.

Communicate your plan before acting.

Henry Hunt

Attention to detail could have made him the ideal accountant. He is reputed as having reminded a cannoneer, who was firing too many cannon balls in the heat of battle, that for each round fired it was costing the United States government two dollars and sixty-seven cents. Before the final attack on July 3, he was heard to say, "Do not waste ammunition, and do not engage small bodies of men." He even calculated how many cannon rounds were expended in the three-day battle: thirty-two thousand, seven hundred and eighty-one.

He was the Chief of Union Artillery. In the final hours of the battle, he had taken the advice of a junior officer that amounted to a clever trap of Lee's infantry. When he saw his enemy counterpart, Porter Alexander, pouring huge amounts of cannon fire on the Union position to little effect, he knew it was a prelude to an offensive infantry attack by the enemy. Hunt reasoned that if he answered Alexander in kind, he would be doing nothing more than depleting his own ammunition supply. The advice he received was to trick Alexander into thinking Hunt no longer had enough firepower, so a cease-fire was ordered. Thirteen years later, Alexander observed: "The Federal batteries were, I thought, most remarkably amiable all that morning..." Alexander never understood what was already in motion.

Hunt discussed his cease-fire strategy with General Hancock, who simply chose to ignore it. Hancock believed that artillery fire was good for the morale of his infantry, perhaps equal to the excitement created by firecrackers on the 4th of July, and proceeded to countermand Hunt's order to keep the cannons silent. Exactly who had command jurisdiction was not clear.

Not one to be distracted, Hunt later countermanded Hancock's order and proceeded to bluff his counterpart by having a few of his cannons taken away to the rear. The bluff worked: Confederate commander Alexander concluded that Hunt was low on ammunition, or simply could not sustain the Union position. Being low on ammunition himself, Alexander urgently recommended to Pickett that he hurry his forces onto the field and commence his attack. With what little ammunition he had left, he could offer only limited support. Hunt's strategy was about to work, but to a point.

Pickett's Charge was in motion. As the Confederates walked across nearly a mile of open field, Hunt unleashed some one hundred and twenty guns in a cannon barrage from several directions. Because of Hancock's previous order to have all cannons firing in immediate response to Alexander, much of Hunt's ammunition supply was already depleted. His cannon fire was not enough to do the damage that could have been done. The primary cause of the problem, Hunt recalled, "was in the obscurity of our army regulations as to the artillery, and the absence of all regulations as to the proper relations of the different arms of the service to one another." In other words, army regulations did not make room for combining responsibilities; it was not a seamless mechanism where the integration of activities was the standard. In spite of antiquated rules of engagement (by modern standards), his artillery contributed to the killing and wounding of over six thousand Rebels in less than an hour. With a veiled attack on these regulations and perhaps on Hancock himself, Hunt wrote later: "Had my instructions been followed...I do not believe that Pickett's division would have reached our lines. We lost...the fire of one-third of our guns...it cost us much blood, lives, and for a moment endangered the success of the battle."

With blurred lines of authority, Hunt's only failure, if there was one, was not convincing Hancock of the merits of his intent. The imperatives of the moment demanded a collaboration that did not exist. To the end, Hunt was the skilled perfectionist: to be certain that each cannon was well-placed and ready, he spent nearly three hours inspecting his forces. If the Devil was in the details, Hunt was everywhere to crush him.

Gettysburg Lessons

Communicate effectively.

You can pay a high price for failing to communicate effectively. Men may have died because Hunt failed to convince Hancock. He could have taken General Hancock aside and stated the benefits of his strategy in no uncertain terms, that his artillery could soften up the enemy lines and make Hancock's own infantry less vulnerable. Hunt proved that if you do not influence someone to your way of thinking, you will be ignored, and the results could be disastrous.

Listen to subordinates.

Good leaders listen. Hunt demonstrated that under great pressure, no matter what your position in life, there is much to be gained from listening to the suggestions of others in lesser positions. Such posture creates an environment of trust that ultimately results in win-win situations. Allow yourself to follow, to be led by positive influences.

Be unpredictable with opponents.

To win a contest you must assess the strengths and weaknesses of your opponent. Hunt knew the strength of the Southern force and proceeded with an imaginative strategy despite restrictive army rules. Sometimes it takes imagination to beat your opponent at his own game, like pretending to make a move in one direction when you are actually going in another. Be unpredictable. Keep your opponent off-guard. Lead your rival to where he does not intend to go by the influence of your imagination.

Simplify.

Hunt could simplify the cost of something so that the common soldier understood. If you allow someone to spend your money, for example, be sure they know and respect your limits. Once you give someone a clear and simple picture of your finances, it will influence them not to treat your money frivolously.

Concentrate on winning.

When Hunt instructed his men not to "engage small bodies of men," it was because he was concentrating his resources (cannon balls and canister shot) on the larger issue of winning. In other words, diluting your resources on the small things will drain what you need to tackle the big things.

Innovate.

Frank Haskell

Once a school superintendent and a town clerk, his administrative expertise qualified him as General Gibbon's primary assistant. No manual on military tactics ever stated that an officer should use his sword as a motivational tool. On horseback he took creative measures to insure that his fellow soldiers would not lose their position or their perspective. Seeing the ground giving way to the Confederates, he saw what appeared to be a mass retreat of Union soldiers not under his command. Recognizing the significance of the Union position and the desperation of the moment, he did not seek permission to act. General Hancock was highly complimentary of Haskell's moves:

> ...at a critical point of the battle, when the contending forces were but 50 or 60 yards apart, believing that an example was necessary, and ready to sacrifice his life, [Haskell] rode between the contending lines with the view of giving encouragement to ours and leading it forward...

Encouragement came in doses of blunt persuasion. To the many frightened men who appeared to be running away, he screamed at them to turn around, hold their ground, and fire back. "The fate of Gettysburg," he wrote with elegant hyperbole, "hung upon a spider's single thread." With an attractive flare for eloquent subtlety, he added: "On some unpatriotic backs of those not quick of comprehension, the flat of my sabre fell not lightly, and at its touch their love of country returned..." By his words, he had a kinder, gentler approach to command. By his actions, he did whatever was necessary to get the job done. The moment was history's cue to demonstrate that the sword was mightier than the oral command.

Perhaps accurately his own commander concluded that Haskell "was a young man on my staff who...did more than any other one man to repulse Pickett's assault at Gettysburg..." History's design for Haskell was to be at the right place at precisely at the right time.

As an appealing footnote to history, he would have made the nineteenth century version of the Guinness Book of World Records. Immediately after the battle, he sat down and wrote what must have been the longest letter ever written, intended for publication in newspapers. Writing with an ordinary pencil, he described for his brother in forty thousand words what he had witnessed.

Gettysburg Lessons

Innovate.

Some problems defy ordinary textbook solutions. Under pressure you have the ability to think of solutions that challenge the standard, demonstrating that innovation can do more to influence your progress than traditional formulas for problem-solving. Haskell saw something that did not look right and influenced the outcome. He did not have to ask anyone what to do. Necessity forced him to invent measures to accomplish the task at hand.

Do it yourself.

Without being asked, take the initiative as Haskell did: do not wait for someone else to solve pressing problems. Plus, greater self-esteem follows accomplishment. Take on a project you are not expected to handle - any project. It can be helping a co-worker, washing your mother's kitchen floor, making an unscheduled delivery, even cleaning your room. Do anything that does not fall into your daily routine. It will influence you to look at things with a different and fresh perspective. Surprise yourself with creative solutions you discover by yourself.

Keep your promises.

John Gibbon

He swore an oath. It was a sacred statement of obligation. As a Union army officer who grew up in the South, he swore to preserve, protect, and defend his country. Once he raised his right hand, he knew that he was making an intensely personal statement about who he was, that he was obligating himself to whatever demands were made by that oath. An oath was his uncompromising personal guarantee. He was keenly aware that he was putting duty above recognition and honor above reputation. So personal was his oath that it meant placing country above the love of his own family. He took an especially disheartening rebuke from his three brothers and two brothers-in-law: they disowned him and went off to fight for the Confederacy.

He was very strict, and his men respected his judgment. When they would come under attack, he would be there to steady them. He could be found strolling slowly up and down a line under fire as if he were a walking bomb shelter. In this battle he was heard to say, "Let them come up close before you fire, and then aim low and steadily." No one could tell that he was frightened out of his wits. "Of course, it would be absurd," he later wrote, "to say we were not scared." Like any other human being in a tense and deadly situation, he had flashing thoughts of his family. Just before the bombardment of the third day that would hit his line directly, he scribbled a note to his wife that typically began with, "My darling mama."

He respected his foe. Having received a shoulder wound and carried from the field before the end of the third day's battle, he twice praised his adversary with phrases like, "the enemy's fire and the noble manner in which it was sustained," or their front line excited "the admiration of every one." Ultimately, he felt it his duty to tell his men, by his brave example, that danger had to be mocked and the task at hand had to be completed. He wrote an incisive comment about the greatest need of the moment: "Few acquainted with the rigid requirements of discipline and of how an efficient military organization must necessarily be a machine which works by the will of one man...can appreciate the importance of drill and discipline in a crisis..."

Gettysburg Lessons

Keep your promises.

Words are vessels that carry intent to their destination. When you make a promise, whether you put it in the form of a written contract, or you say it out loud in taking an oath, someone is depending on you. Someone is expecting you to do what you promised. When you fulfill your promises, you influence others to trust you. That opens you to all kinds of opportunities. You can be your own promise-keeper: meet your deadlines, complete your projects, and create a habit that will make you feel positive about yourself. Promises are sacred influences that lead to valued outcomes.

Planning eliminates a lot of fear.

It is okay to be scared like Gibbon, especially in the face of unknowns. Plan your success and you will start to feel the excitement. Success entails a few unknowns, such as the world economy changing dramatically overnight. But planning your success does not depend on how the rest of the world is doing. It depends on the influence of solid planning, a belief in your abilities to achieve, a passion for achieving something specific, self-imposed deadlines to meet, and the flexibility to change. Your fears will be harnessed, and you will witness your own progress.

Respect good competitors.

Respect a persistent and talented adversary who is an honorable opponent. Respect is the barometer that measures your coolness and objectivity in dealing with opposition effectively. Respect will influence you to learn how competitors will maneuver their resources and energies around you. With a realistic outlook, you will be able to plan your own moves to successfully counter those which challenge you.

Ideas have power to motivate.

Lewis Armistead

He was expelled from West Point for breaking a plate over the head of fellow cadet, Jubal Early. But in 1839 he was commissioned into the infantry and became a twenty-two-year career officer in the US Army. He came from a family rich in military tradition. In a tearful departure from his dear friend and later battlefield adversary, Winfield Scott Hancock, he joined the Confederate army after his native state of Virginia voted to secede.

He had little patience with civilians who volunteered. He preferred to work with men like himself who were committed to the army as a career. Always blunt with his subordinates, some officers found his manner insulting if not condescending. He had high confidence in his own judgment, refusing an order in a previous battle on the logic that its fulfillment would be a disaster.

Now he was facing a new disaster. Inexplicably, there is no record that he ever challenged his participation in Pickett's Charge, which he considered a mistake. With total resignation, he simply told his men to make this charge "for your wives, your mothers, your sisters, and your sweethearts." His seeming resignation to disaster may be explained by the facts that he was twice a widower, lost two children to disease, and became a loner. On the third day, his mental attitude suffered from lack of sleep, overexertion, and the stress of knowing that death was almost certain. Heat exhaustion from wearing a wool coat in near ninety-degree heat could also have been an aggravating factor affecting his state of mind. Before the charge, he handed over a ring from his finger as a parting gift for George Pickett's fiancé. Armistead was not smiling back at fate.

With tragic irony he and his old friend Hancock were opposing each other on the same field. Armistead had to march approximately three quarters of a mile with Hancock's men waiting to destroy him. He was leading his men proudly with his hat half way down his raised sword. At one point along the way, he remarked to a fellow officer, "Look at my line; it never looked better on dress parade." Another Rebel officer following Armistead commented that no other commander led a desperate charge "with more absolute abandon of self..." In the last minutes of the battle, Armistead was struck down by two bullets not far from where Hancock also lay bleeding. They never saw each other in those final moments of the battle, nor ever again. Armistead died two days later.

Gettysburg Lessons

Ideas have power to motivate.

Those who followed Armistead were following someone who held on to an abstraction, an idea that motivated their behavior for a cause greater than themselves. He demonstrated that an abstraction can have far greater influence over behavior than individuals who have authority. Promoting a powerful idea enables you to lead by its influence, and ideas that influence are what make followers leaders.

Believe in yourself.

Richard Garnett

Despite the support of his own men, who were convinced that he had been misjudged and unnecessarily reprimanded by a previous senior commander, he felt the need to regain his self-respect. Garnett apparently believed that a demonstration of unusual valor would give him redemption. He made a fateful decision on the third day of the battle: though he could not walk after being kicked by his own horse, he rode his stallion into the most devastating enemy fire of the entire battle, Pickett's Charge.

He appeared calm and deliberate, convincing his men to close ranks even as they were being slaughtered at every step along the way. Contrary to his own self-image, one of his officers observed: "He was a noble specimen of manhood and was greatly admired by those who knew him." Earlier he told General Armistead that the upcoming charge "...was a desperate thing to attempt." Pickett told him, "Dick, old fellow,...I advise you to get across those fields as quick as you can, for in my opinion you are going to catch hell!" Nonetheless, he remained on his horse and as the perfect target continued to encourage his men to move forward. "There was scarcely an officer or man in the command," a wounded Rebel officer wrote, "whose attention was not attracted by the cool and handsome bearing of General Garnett...."

Hell came ferociously as Garnett's men marched towards their own butchery. Redemption, if their commander needed it, was purchased with the ultimate sacrifice. "Just as the General turned his horse's head slightly to the left," wrote a Rebel private, "he was struck in the head by a rifle or musket ball and fell dead from his horse."

Because souvenir collectors were among the Union troops who took boots, swords and insignia from the dead after the battle, Garnett's body was never identified. The only items that could be recognized as belonging to Garnett were a watch and a sword, and they were not discovered until some years later in a Baltimore pawnshop.

Gettysburg Lessons

Believe in yourself.

Write a list of those things you do best. Proclaim them to yourself boldly and passionately. Put the list in a conspicuous place so you can see them everyday. By its influence it will spark your enthusiasm to establish goals and sustain belief that you can achieve them. Garnett did not have to die to prove he was fearless anymore than you have to risk your life in a dangerous activity to prove yourself to others.

Beware of self-limiting beliefs.

Garnett is a prime example of not heeding the Shakespearean maxim, "Discretion is the better part of valor." Desperate people often do desperate things. Yet those who perceive themselves as desperate even in the face of contrary evidence can ruin themselves. A negative perception of yourself is nothing more than a self-imposed set of self-limiting beliefs. Those beliefs can lead to self-destructive behavior.

We all make wrong decisions. Share your learning experiences, including your mistakes, with those whose judgment you respect. Personal growth awaits you.

Appreciate your talents.

Garnett forced himself to choose between finding honor and staying alive. It was the most extreme choice because he put his life at extraordinary risk. Although you may never experience such a stressful moment as Garnett, recognize such moments of choice as a time to discover who you are, giving you opportunity to inventory your talents and use them to your best advantage.

Persistence pays.

Alonzo Cushing

He once remarked in a letter to his soldier-brother William what could summarize the effectiveness of the Union army before Gettysburg: "The fighting has been terrific but as usual void of results."

He could trace his roots to John and Priscilla Alden of the *Mayflower*. With a Puritan pedigree, his was a heritage of patriots who always answered the call to defend their country. With ethnic and religious prejudices so prevalent in this period of the nation's history, Cushing had no trouble working with heavily-accented Germans or men with thick Irish brogues. They reciprocated with a great deal of admiration for their young commander.

He still looked like a boy at the age of twenty-two. Having proven his courage on other fields of battle, he did not allow his youthful appearance to stand in the way of his desire to succeed. Perhaps to add some semblance of manhood to his image, occasionally he could be seen smoking a pipe or a cigar.

He was planted squarely in the middle of the most dangerous moments of the battle. When a small group of cannoneers panicked, Cushing drew his revolver and screamed, "...come back to your post! The first man who leaves his post again I'll blow his brains out!" While assisting his cannoneers with loading their guns, they were quickly falling wounded and dead. One particular gun was overheating, and the escaping gases from the barrel burned his thumb to the bone. The pain was unbearable. Suddenly two bullets hit him, one in his right shoulder and one in his stomach area. Seconds later he suffered a direct shrapnel blast to his groin. Bleeding profusely and in excruciating pain, Cushing was going into shock, but somehow continued to give orders that could hardly be heard in the deafening noise of overworked muskets and cannons. His sergeant begged him to go to the rear. Cushing refused, barely uttering the words, "There's no time...I stay right here and fight it out, or die in the attempt.... I'll give them one more shot!" With one hand firmly committed to stopping his own bleeding, he continued to direct the firing of whatever shells he had left.

In addition to his brutal wounds, his life ended when a bullet entered through his mouth and plowed a path to the back of his brain. Cushing's singular effort became another brave contribution to the success of his team, the Union army. His fighting had been terrific, but not void of results.

Gettysburg Lessons

Persistence pays.

In addition to exploding artillery shells at the enemy, Cushing exploded perceptions of all those who knew him. He performed with persistence because of his commitment to winning. Cushing also illustrates that although your appearance may have you feeling insecure, your sense of commitment and responsibility may prove to be your ticket to safety, your way out of a jam, your resolution of a conflict, your solution to a problem, or winning a victory in the face of impossible odds. Some influences are neatly disguised.

Place no limits on yourself.

Unlike Cushing most people place limitations on themselves with such thoughts as, "I don't look old enough for this job," or, "I'm not educated enough." However, like Cushing, successful people will overcompensate for deficiencies and succeed. Abraham Lincoln had less than a year of formal education, but he mastered the English language enough to leave us the most powerful speeches ever written to sustain the world's greatest constitutional republic.

Confide in someone you trust.

Look for positive people to keep you motivated. That is what Cushing did for his men. Positive people may be another teammate, a coworker, or a spouse. These are people who do not think of themselves as leaders, but demonstrate leadership's most fundamental quality, influencing those around them to think and act positively. They say an encouraging word, enough for you to make that extra effort. Recognize your own individual ability to influence others for better outcomes in their daily lives. Good employers, good teachers, good friends, good parents, and good children do it every day.

Life is not fair.

Cushing was young, brave, determined, and admired. Yet he was struck down viciously in his prime. Like so many soldiers on the field that day, he suffered under no illusion that nothing adverse would happen to him. If you understand that bad things can happen to you, and you take responsibility for the mistakes you make, you will never think of yourself as a victim.

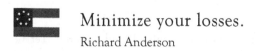

Minimize your losses.

Richard Anderson

He was a modest and amiable general when self-promotion and boastfulness were so characteristic of the officer class in both armies. His strong moral character made him one of the favorite officers in the Rebel army. After more than twenty years as a career soldier, he was honored by the state of South Carolina for his bravery in the Mexican War. General Lee complimented "Fighting Dick" by calling this forty-two-year-old subordinate a "noble old soldier." Anderson never boasted of his accomplishments, but some of his junior officers resented his omissions of their combat achievements in his official reports.

On the second day at Gettysburg, Anderson's behavior was peculiar and uncharacteristic of a talented general. He was not paying close attention to the activity of his own forces. Communications broke down with one of his commanders, claiming that had Anderson "...seen with his own eyes" what was happening on the field, the battle could have turned out favorably for the South.

Anderson mistakenly set up his headquarters in a location that was not in view of his units, making it impossible to see how he ought to coordinate their movements. An aide to his superior later accused Anderson of "indolence," but dereliction of duty would have been more accurate. When a messenger from another general's staff rushed to seek Anderson's assistance, he found Anderson and his staff in a carefree posture, seemingly oblivious to the gravity of the situation. Anderson's inattention was the sand in the lubricated engine of Lee's attack plan that thwarted victory on the second day. No explanation was ever given as to why, but uncharacteristic of many generals, Anderson willingly accepted responsibility for his behavior.

Gettysburg Lessons

Pay attention.

When you are not paying attention to what is required of you, as Anderson demonstrated, you are less effective. To minimize your mistakes, prioritize and prepare for maximum results. You also need something in reserve in case of the unexpected. Anticipating is following influences that allow you to perform well.

Lose by failing to lead.

Get involved with those you manage. Let everyone know you are concerned, aware, and taking charge. Anderson neglected his obligation, or did not take it seriously enough. When everyone sees that you mean business, you are having an influence on them to achieve desired outcomes.

Communicate positively and often.
Alexander Hays

This Union general could have sold tickets for front-row seats to the battle. His enthusiasm for combat was so intense that his version of a warning of pending danger was this excited announcement: "Now, boys, you will see some fun!" One New York colonel observed with affection that Hays could be found "where danger was the greatest, where the bullets flew the thickest, where the fighting was the fiercest..." Sensitive to what he believed was a uniform misperception of him, he complained: "It is intimated that I am too fond of fighting which is as ridiculously absurd as many other reports of me." Like it or not, he understood that his incessant blasts of kinetic energy crafted a high profile. What he did not understand, or ignored, was his identity with the soldier's ultimate compliment: a junior officer remarked that Hays "offered the rare gift of inspiring his men."

A Congressman's son, a gold-digger in California, an athlete and a civil engineer, "Fighting Alex" spent months in a hospital for a severe wound in a previous battle. With a muscular drive to achieve results, some of his men despised him, and many of his peer commanders considered him arrogant. Being a hearty and vigorous showman to motivate his men, he never forgot that using sound judgment was paramount. Not unlike most other commanders, he was always the coach encouraging his men to get their work done. During the battle's worst moments, Hays was heard shouting, "They are coming, boys!" "We must whip them!" "Hurrah! Boys, we're giving them hell!"

Hays was a native Pennsylvanian, so he took Gettysburg personally. "I was fighting for my native state," this emotional commander remarked, "and before I went in thought of those at home I so dearly love." He succeeded in communicating his emotions to those he led, and they in turn declared that they would follow him "to the death."

As the Confederates were marching across the fields toward his line without firing a shot, Hays had his men occupy this pregnant moment with ordinary drill to keep their minds off the inevitable. It was an ingenious communication specifically designed to get his men "back to basics," to physically feel and manipulate their rifles just before they would be ordered to use them.

When his units rose up and annihilated the approaching Confederates, one Union private observed Hays for having "...cheered our skirmishers, who were driving the Rebels before them." But the battle was taking its toll: he lost two horses and thirteen orderlies were either killed or wounded. When his fight was over, to show utter contempt for his enemy, he ordered an aide to fetch him a Rebel flag so he could drag it on the ground along his entire line. His men threw their caps high in the air, as one aide recalled, "showing their admiration for their glorious division commander..." Filing a story about Hayes after the battle, a news reporter wished everyone "...to honor him as the bravest of soldiers and love him as the best hearted of men." In the excitement of the moment of victory, Hays reached for one of his aides and gave him a kiss.

Gettysburg Lessons

Communicate positively and often.
The most effective way to influence is to act like Alexander Hays. He was a master motivator. He always made his men feel terrific about what they were doing, and he made every effort to do it often. To have the most productive relationship with your children, your spouse, your associates, your employees, or your customers, communicate positively and often.

Be enthusiastic.
To be effective, you must believe in what you say and do. Effective people "see some fun" in what they contribute, in what they sell, and in what they want to accomplish. They never lose sight of their objective. They always transfer to others what cannot be taught in business schools - enthusiasm, a driving energy, a passion that drives you to succeed. It puts fun in what you do. In the results department, enthusiasm will nearly always beat out an impressive academic credential.

Enthusiasm is easily communicated. If you want someone to get excited about something, show your own excitement. It is contagious leading. It allows you to do what Hays did - mobilize others to perform demanding tasks that they believed could not be done. Point out product features, personality traits, company benefits, new ideas - anything beneficial that causes you to have enthusiasm and be an influence. To really drive the point home, add some animated body language when you speak.

To make your subordinates more productive, cheer them warmly and frequently. When they do a good job, credit them publicly. Hays treated his men like family. They responded in kind because people will give back what you give. Enthusiasm is the emotional steroid that invigorates you to get what you want. Once a goal is achieved, you are energized to go on to your next achievement. Enthusiasm is your success in motion.

Practice the basics.

Before his men were about to engage the enemy, Hays made sure his troops practiced the basic duties of being a soldier. Following someone's influence to practice the basics makes you more proficient.

Great organizations and great leaders create each other.

A great leader exercises minimal control when she or he has talented employees doing the actual work, particularly in a trusting environment. Doing what everyone does best has a positive influence on outcomes. A culture of trust is what makes good followers leaders and good leaders followers.

Back off to try again.

Theodore Ellis

Somebody had something he wanted. He saw enemy soldiers occupying a house and a nearby barn, so he sought to capture and occupy those structures. Knowing that he and his men would be fired on, they rushed the farm and succeeded in clearing out the Confederates. There was just one problem: a Rebel artillerist watching from a distance wanted to use Ellis and his men for target practice. One Rebel later wrote of this moment as a "leisurely" exercise. The name of the farm mocked the killing activity that was unfolding - the Bliss farm. Once the cannonade began, they ran out of the house and into the barn.

After setting the house on fire, Ellis and his Connecticut survivors escaped to safety. Retreat became a stimulating option. Escaping with their wounded and dead was the better part of valor, and it allowed them to fight another day.

The Confederates were expending an inordinate amount of artillery into the barn, not saving their ammunition for the charge that had to be made later that afternoon. In a small way Ellis's brave action to take the farm contributed to the depletion of precious ammunition that was needed by Confederate artillery on the third day.

During the final charge of the Rebels, Ellis's men were able to break the lines in front of them faster than on any other part of the line. That was because many of his men were armed with breech-loading rifles instead of muskets, which enabled them to fire more bullets in a shorter period of time.

Gettysburg Lessons

Back off to try again.

Succeeding can mean things going wrong through no fault of your own, as they did for Ellis once he was in possession of the barn. When your achievement is melting away and uncontrollable events are causing you to rethink what you did, do not try to overcome what you cannot. Recognition of what you have accomplished will give you renewed confidence in your abilities to take new directions. Establish a new goal, and given the "bad" experience you had, you have a premium possession - experience, a great influence that gives you more ability, wider perspective and much-needed confidence to adapt to new circumstances.

Guard your assets.

When you expend resources as frivolously as the Confederates did on Ellis, you will waste assets. You cannot buy a new car if you have just enough money to pay your current bills. You cannot go to the college of your choice if you spend all of your free time playing a guitar. You cannot be an ideal parent if you spend your spare time in career-related activities. Not concentrating your talents on a necessary goal will guarantee failure. It also calls into question the desire you really had to achieve the goal in the first place. Talent is so easy to waste when there is no goal to influence you to achieve.

Take precautions against the unexpected.

Take precautions for unexpected events. If you become sick, you ought to have health insurance so as not to drain the money you already have. Always have something in reserve for something you cannot anticipate. This will make sure you do not touch money you have allocated for two great influences on your actions - education and retirement.

Compete with better resources.

To defeat your competitor, tilt the odds in your favor. Ellis had a faster-loading rifle that enabled him to break his foe with confidence.

You can do the impossible.

Judson Kilpatrick

He was a West Point grad, a widower and a talented cavalryman. In his youth he became an avid reader and admirer of great military figures in history. This interest developed into an intense desire to be a soldier, which won the support of his entire family.

With a flare for acting, at age seventeen he made political speeches for a Congressional candidate who later endorsed him for his appointment to West Point. "With unwavering good-nature and ready repartee," wrote his roommate and class-elected valedictorian of five-feet, seven-inches and one hundred and forty pounds, "Kilpatrick met all the harmless humor and practical jokes of the corps, and, as time rolled on, won the esteem of his classmates and respect of his instructors."

Having married immediately after graduation, he left for the battlefields and became the first regular army officer to be wounded in the Civil War. Despite back pains from a kidney disease that would kill him years later, he distinguished himself so quickly in subsequent battles that he was promoted from lieutenant to "Boy General" at age twenty-five. Success and youth were not incompatible.

When he arrived at Gettysburg, he had to deal with a commander whose orders not only depleted Kilpatrick's own forces, but reflected ignorance of rocky terrain over which his cavalry could not be effective against an enemy of superior numbers. With an objective that was diversionary, his commander ordered him to "fire all your guns, charge in their rear, make a strong diversion."

Kilpatrick was being ordered to do the impossible. With treacherous ground and a lack of support mechanisms that would have demoralized other commanders, Kilpatrick could have followed a strict interpretation of his orders and led a thoughtless charge with dire consequences. Instead, he took his time to devise a creative alternative attack plan without changing the original. One can only imagine the stream of self-questioning that influenced how and where he was going to attack. Perhaps the toughest question for Kilpatrick was, "Facing an enemy in a better position and with greater numbers, how can I create a weakness where there is none?"

He ordered his subordinate commanders to charge enemy artillery (not infantry as his orders specified), which created a weakness in the Rebel line of infantry by stretching it, forcing the enemy commander to divert a goodly amount of his troops to deal with Kilpatrick. The plan worked, and by Civil War standards it precipitated an extraordinarily low casualty rate of only three percent. His superiors were impressed with his results, and after the battle his men gave him a new sword as a token of their admiration. "He organized carefully as he approached the enemy," wrote one general who admired Kilpatrick's fighting style, and "was very rapid in his movements, showing unusual dash in attacks and extraordinary celerity and dexterity in extricating himself from an unsuccessful foray. I doubt if any other officer could, with his fewness of numbers, have rendered the army at all times more effective service." Kilpatrick could well be today's role model for every US Army commando who likes to say, "The difficult we do immediately, the impossible takes a little longer."

Gettysburg Lessons

You can do the impossible.

Sometimes we find ourselves in impossible situations where there appears to be no way out, as Kilpatrick discovered. When failure appears obvious, Kilpatrick proved there can be other options even if you find them unattractive. The impossible is what forced Kilpatrick to imagine a better plan. He would not entertain the possibility of defeat. Kilpatrick's new plan, which came from looking beyond the limitations of his orders and trusting his vision of what could be done, influenced him to achieve the objective he was assigned. Leadership is following your own vision.

Stay focused.

David Gregg

Public service was a tradition in the Gregg family. David was the first cousin to the Governor of Pennsylvania, and his paternal grandfather was a member of Congress for more than twenty years in the early part of the nineteenth century. Before coming east to serve in the war, Gregg was stationed in California.

He was unruffled in a tense and deadly situation. General Gregg was known to drag on his pipe and tell his men to remain calm no matter how dangerous the moment. Boldness and ruthlessness were common adjectives to describe prominent cavalry officers, but such words never defined Gregg's style. He made self-control a hallmark of his leadership.

He treasured his anonymity and kept the media at a distance. He never wore a plumed hat or a velvet uniform, which were considered standard features of attire for cavalry officers. Unlike the flamboyant J.E.B. Stuart or George Custer, thirty-two-year-old Gregg had no colorful traits to which newspapermen could dedicate a barrel of ink. When the horseshoe met the trail, his concentration was on results, not on making a dashing impression.

On the third day, his deliberate and calm demeanor assured that the most respected cavalry officer in the Confederacy, J.E.B. Stuart, would not win a victory. Instead, the cavalry battle ended in a draw, but not before Gregg was faced with a sudden crisis in command. A cavalry unit on loan to him had just received orders to relocate to another field position as Gregg was going into battle. Gregg instructed the commander to ignore his orders until the fight was over. Making few mistakes in battle, Gregg's courage on this day earned him the position of the chief cavalry officer of the Union's largest army.

Gettysburg Lessons

Stay focused.

Like Gregg, pay no attention to fluff and flattery; they will distract you. The result you work for - your goal - is the influence that will keep you focused and clear-headed about what has to be done.

Concentrate on results, not tasks.

Another way of staying focused is not to concentrate on tasks. They will keep you from seeing the big picture of your responsibilities.

Self-control inspires confidence.

Good leaders like Gregg have self-control, a quality that influences others to follow your example.

Accept change.
Wesley Culp

His story is one of the great ironies of the Civil War. Born and raised in Gettysburg, he relocated with his Gettysburg employer to Virginia in 1857. When the war began he was living only forty-two miles away from his birthplace while maintaining in constant contact with his family. His Southern home gave him cause to become a Confederate soldier; it was simply a matter of repelling the invader and nothing more. Because of his small size and lack of a Southern accent, he was nicknamed, "the little Yank."

Before going into battle it was standard procedure for a general to round up any soldiers who may have been former residents of the area, to use them as guides. Culp was never asked even when his Gettysburg origins were discovered.

He visited his sister one evening who warned him that some relatives would shoot him if he were discovered. After a lengthy conversation, he departed with the promise that he would return the next day. Culp was killed the following morning, not far from his second cousin's property, known as Culp's Hill, where he grew up and played as a boy.

Legend has it that another tragic irony was in the making before the battle. Confederate Culp found his brother William as a Union prisoner. The reality of their meeting was stark and troubling: two brothers found themselves on opposite sides. At the time of this reunion, Wesley was introduced to William's wounded friend from Gettysburg, Jack Skelley, who asked Wesley to deliver a message to a lady friend if he ever got to Gettysburg. Culp was unable to play the role of messenger because he was killed on the same day as the recipient of the message, the only civilian to be killed at Gettysburg, Jennie Wade. Skelley died nine days later of his wounds. He never knew if she received his message and she never knew one was coming.

Gettysburg Lessons

Expect your convictions to be tested.

Culp was prepared for the most severe test of his commitment to the South. Despite coming back to fight on the fields of his youth, he never retreated from that commitment. When you make a pledge to someone, to an idea, or to a goal, be prepared for your commitment to be tested severely. To pass the test takes Culp Courage, which can be the most difficult way to influence.

Accept change.

"Home" is a four-letter world the heart never leaves, the magnetic influence that keeps drawing us back, but whatever meaning you attach to it, time and events will change it without your consent, as it did for Wesley Culp.

Live by your convictions.

Sister Camilla O'Keefe, Catholic Nun

The day after the battle Sister Camilla and fifteen other Sisters of Charity of St. Vincent de Paul arrived in Gettysburg to begin a different battle with no illusions - attempt to save the lives of at least twenty thousand wounded. In her own narrative of the scene she observed that the wounded were strewn all over the battlefield and in homes, barns, town buildings, schools, and churches. "Many of them lay in their own blood," she wrote, "and the water used for bathing their wounds, but no word of complaint escaped their lips."

A genuine ecumenical attitude was in the making, one that expressed a united effort by people of different religious beliefs. The Commissary head supplying Sister Camilla with clothing and food was so impressed with her charitable attitude toward the wounded of both North and South that he expressed the hope that one day "we shall worship at the same altar together."

She and the other Sisters were required by one of their vows to be obedient, making it easier for the surgeons to get things done in a hurry. By caring for the wounded of both armies, she became partly responsible for reducing the prejudices against Catholicism to the point that many of those treated were baptized into the religion. One recovering Confederate prisoner remarked, "Goodbye Sisters, we are going to prison now, but it would not be prison, if we had you to go along and minister to our wants of soul and body."

Gettysburg Lessons

Live by your convictions.

Living by your convictions will influence people to imitate you. Your actions may convert some to your way of thinking, as did Sister Camilla's behavior. You have the inherent ability to lead others simply by the way you live.

You can be extraordinary.

Helen Gilson

Orphaned as a teenager she became the governess to her uncle's children. Trained as a care-giver she helped organize a local Boston chapter of the Soldier's Aid Society at the war's outbreak when she was twenty-five years of age.

Once she arrived on the battlefields she did not see people as black or white, or dressed in blue or gray. Anyone who was wounded from North or South deserved equal care and tenderness. She even suggested that the song she wanted to sing in front of the wounded at Gettysburg, *When This Cruel War Is Over*, would appeal to both sides. Empathy ruled over her every action. A member of the Sanitary Commission described her caring for wounded Rebels "upon heaps of manure...tormented with vermin, their wounds still undressed, and many longing for amputation..." because the pain was unbearable. Someone else suggested "that no one could watch her long without becoming lyrical and dewy-eyed." Everyone acknowledged that an uncommon if not holy person was among them.

Contrabands, as runaway slaves were called, would be treated with equality and dignity. She single-handedly taught them how to tend to and care for the wounded as a nurse's assistant. She made efficient use of their time, allowing them to contribute their efforts to her mission. (One can only imagine how she affected the racial prejudices of white soldiers who were nursed back to good health by her black aids.) In return, she was accorded great respect and cooperation. Her accomplishment of mobilizing so many for her single purpose was considered the ideal example of how other Union army hospitals should respond when runaways appeared on the scene.

She cared for hundreds of wounded every month, listened to the cries of the dying every hour, and endured the threat of disease every minute. She remained a deeply religious woman. Her commitment was a prayer in progress, which may explain why and how she persisted in a manner reminiscent of the Rule of Saint Dominic: *To work is to pray.*

Gettysburg Lessons

You can be extraordinary.

Helen Gilson demonstrated that we are capable of great acts of compassion. She was able to rise above the ordinary drudgeries of the moment to perform extraordinary acts on a daily basis. She was motivated by what she believed, a powerful influence that led her to care for the needs of the sick and dying. Being motivated by something higher than yourself - finding ways to improve the lives of people you do not know - propels you to accomplish exceptional deeds. It is one of the noblest ways to influence.

Never be afraid to seek help.

When you are determined to reach your goal, enlist those whose help you will need to achieve it. When you are scrupulously fair to everyone along the way, people are disposed to help you accomplish your objectives. Be open to the most unexpected sources of help, for they may play a valuable part in your future.

Be a source of inspiration.

Like Helen Gilson you can be a source of inspiration by influencing others to perform similar actions.

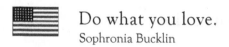

Do what you love.

Sophronia Bucklin

She could have declared war as the great equalizer of the sexes. She suggested in her own book that it was as much a woman's duty to restore a wounded soldier to health as it was for a soldier to restore a divided country to union.

She joined the Union army as a nurse, and it raised hostility against her only because she was identified with "the government" - someone not to be trusted. The animosity came from miscreant officers, and army surgeons saw fit to fire her several times for being too generous with supplying the needs of the wounded. Society's oppressive attitude toward women at the time only added to the hostility toward Bucklin, or any female who stood head and shoulders above any white males.

In spite of the bitterness that assaulted her from her own superiors, she was able to maintain an attitude of compassion for the dying. In fact, she referred to the wounded on stretchers as "each [stretcher] bearing a hero." Then she penned this horrific account: "...at one place, so close that it touched me, hung a sleeve of faded army blue – a dead hand protruding from the worn and blackened cuff – I could not but feel a momentary shudder." She went on to describe what a Hollywood screen writer could envision for a blockbuster horror movie:

Boots, with a leg and foot putrefying within, lay beside the pathway, and ghastly heads, too – over the exposed skulls of which insects crawled – while great worms bored through the rotting eyeballs. Astride a tree sat a bloody horror, with head and limbs severed by shells, the birds having banquetted on it, while the tattered uniform, stained with gore, fluttered dismally in the summer air.

After living with the grotesque aftermath of war, she came to understand the difference between *need* and *want*. She was easily satisfied by the simplest comfort when relief was nowhere to be found. And when she was near death with typhoid fever, she believed that her "love of life had its hidden advantages over death." She lived until 1902, nearly 40 years after army surgeons wistfully declared her imminent death.

Gettysburg Lessons

Do what you love.

Bucklin discovered that one of life's greatest joys is doing what you love, and knowing that it matters. All successful people have this love in common. This is the easiest, surest, and most enjoyable way to influence others. It is not the size of your bank account that makes you happy, it is what you love to do that determines the size to your bank account.

Act on your beliefs.

When you are convinced of a belief that is good for others as well as for yourself, act on it and you will be productive in ways you never dreamed possible. People will be influenced by your behavior. But there will be those who will criticize you for being unconventional and even discourage you from what you want to achieve. When you seek advice to succeed, trust the counsel - the influence - of strangers who are experts in the field of your interest, someone already succeeding at what you want to do.

Be a self-improvement project.

A hostile environment will motivate you to seek new surroundings. If that is not possible, as was the case with Bucklin, look for ways to improve your value to those around you. Becoming better at what you enjoy improves your chances for more opportunities elsewhere. Constant self-improvement will influence someone to recruit, value, or reward your talents.

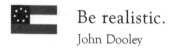

Be realistic.

John Dooley

He was the nineteen-year-old son of a wealthy Irish immigrant. Known as "Gentleman Jack" and an aspirant to the Catholic priesthood, he was convinced that he had to leave his Jesuit college studies to preserve slavery because his family owned so many slaves. Having been jolted by the realities of war in previous battles, he was not beyond self-deprecation as he admitted readily to being "the newest and most ignorant officer in the Regiment." During the sun-baked and fear-drenched death march across an open field on the third day, his only protective shield was a naive hope that somehow doing his duty would miraculously keep him from harm. It was miraculous that he was not killed but merely wounded and taken prisoner.

While a detainee he drew attention to himself by reminding his Union captors of his own Confederate patriotism. If he could not fight with his musket, he was naïve enough to believe that he could fight with his tongue. His verbal slights were met with universal indifference.

His diary reflected a great sense of realism after being wounded in both thighs: "I tell you, there is no romance in making one of those charges...and instead of burning to avenge the insults of our country [the South]...the thought is most frequently, Oh, if I could just come out of this charge safely how thankful would I be!"

Dooley reflected on a surgeon's response to his request to treat his friend, a wounded prisoner with a half-buried shell in his chest. When the doctor promised to look at the wound after he had a chance to eat, Dooley wrote: "Oh humanity! A human life for a cup of coffee!" Dooley's wounds were not treated for six days when maggots began to infest his legs. He never fully recovered, yet continued his studies for the priesthood after the war. He died nine months before his scheduled ordination.

Gettysburg Lessons

Be realistic.

Dooley's youthful idealism took a severe beating in the face of stubborn realism. Allow idealism to be tempered by the influence of experience, leading you to recall that "there is no romance in making one of those charges." Going into a known stressful situation with nothing but hope is a recipe for disaster. Rarely will you think of everything, but careful planning will be the influence that leads you away from situations that have grave consequences, like losing your home, your job, or your family.

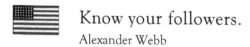

Know your followers.

Alexander Webb

Known to his superior at Gettysburg for being "the most conscientious, hard working and fearless young officer," he was promoted rapidly for being an efficient staff officer. Once challenged with command of the Irish Philadelphia Brigade, this undisciplined group did not take kindly to their new spit-and-polish commander. Preferring to do things by the book, he made a most unusual pact with his men: he would shoot any man who did not carry out his orders and they were to do the same with him. Although it was a self-serving but risky gesture, for the moment at least, words were feeble evidence of his courage.

Webb was promoted to general one week before the great battle. He was largely unknown when he arrived at Gettysburg to take command of four regiments. Obscurity would hinder him at the most inopportune moment. "My men did not know me," Webb wrote to his wife after the battle. "It was necessary to establish myself. They were to be made to feel that I ordered no men to go where I would not go myself." Scared witless during the cannonade, he was seen smoking a cigar and standing with an air of indifference. A deliberate display of a commander's calmness usually had the effect of keeping soldiers steady and focused on their purpose.

At the very height of the Confederate assault on Webb's position, a gap was opening in his line. Many of his frightened troops became instant fugitives. Becoming desperate and ignoring the chain of command, Webb ordered a reserve regiment to attack. With the noise of battle, the men could barely hear him. More frustrating to Webb's intention was their inability to recognize who he was, and by extension, his authority. At the worst possible moment, he was now in command, not of the undecided, but of the unwilling.

The Union gap appeared to be widening, which could result in a Confederate victory. Disgusted and ignoring the danger around him, with a near certainty about his meeting with destiny, Webb *walked* back to the front only to be grazed by a bullet. Witnessing his almost effortless valor, Webb's reluctant men began to open fire in his support.

In a matter of minutes the fate of a country changed, in part by the conspicuous bravery of this young New Yorker who had no previous combat experience as a general. Able to repel a vicious onslaught, Webb was later awarded the Medal of Honor. With an observation that would be difficult to dispute for its understatement, he told his wife: "No general ever had to depend upon his individual exertions than I had."

In his final report of the battle and in the euphoria of victory, instead of rebuking these hesitant reserves, he simply remarked that they "fought steadily and persistently..." His men were now "a real fighting brigade which has learned to obey me implicitly."

Gettysburg Lessons

Know your followers.
Like Webb, those you lead should see you up close and personal, get a measure of you, and sense your commitment to them. You may be a talented manager or parent, but you stand to get more from individuals with a clearer sense of who you are and where you intend to lead them. Webb's famous walk back to danger was a visual influence that helped Webb save the day. Under stressful conditions, good leadership quickly creates good followship.

Trust yourself.
Webb's resolve may be hard to comprehend, but when everything seems to be falling apart, you can forge ahead when you set your mind to expect success. It is the expectation that will influence your progress. Webb's thoughts may well have been expressed in his dramatic walk back to greater danger, which was a totally unexpected behavior pattern in a chaotic situation. It influenced his unwilling troops to respond positively.

Bibliography

Books

Alleman, Tillie Pierce. *At Gettysburg or What A Girl Saw and Heard of the Battle*. W. Lake Borland, New York, 1889.

Bearss, Edwin C. *Fields of Honor*, National Geographic Society, Washington, DC, 2006.

Block, Peter. *The Empowered Manager*, Jossey-Bass Publishers, 1991.

Boritt, Gabor S., Editor. *The Gettysburg Nobody Knows*, Oxford University Press, New York, 1997.

Bowden and Ward. *Last Chance for Victory*, Da Capo Press, 2001.

Bucklin, Sophronia. *In Hospital and Camp*. John E. Potter, Philadelphia, 1869.

Brockett & Vaughn. *Women's Work In The Civil War*, RH Curran, Boston, MA 1867.

Brown, Kent M. *Cushing At Gettysburg*, University of Kentucky Press, 1993.

Carter, Robert G. *Four Brothers in Blue or Sunshine and Shadows of the War of the Rebellion* (Wash., DC, Press of Gibson Brothers, Inc., 1913; reprint, Austin, TX: The University of Texas, 1978).

Coco, Gregory A. *On the Bloodstained Field*, Thomas Publications, 1987.

Conklin, Eileen. *Women at Gettysburg 1863*. Thomas Publications, Gettysburg, 1993.

Coddington, Edwin B. *The Gettysburg Campaign, A Study in Command*. Touchstone, New York, 1968.

Davis, Walter, Editor. *The Image of War: 1861-1865, The Embattled Confederacy*, Volume 3. Doubleday, Garden City, NY, 1982.

Desjardin, Thomas A. *Stand Firm Ye Boys From Maine*, Thomas Publications, Gettysburg, 1995.

Downey, Fairfax. *The Guns at Gettysburg*, D. McKay Co., NY, 1958.

Early, J.A. *War Memoirs*, Indiana University Press, Bloomington, 1960.
230

Fishel, Edwin C. *The Secret War for the Union*, Houghton Mifflin, NY, 1996.

Foote, Shelby. *The Civil War A Narrative Frederickburg to Meridian*. Random House, New York, 1963.

Freeman, Douglas S. *Lee's Lieutenants: A Study in Command*, Volumes 1-3, New York, 1944.

Gallagher, Gary, ed. *The First Day at Gettysburg*, Kent State University Press, 1992.

_____ , ed. *The Third Day at Gettysburg & Beyond*, University of North Carolina, 1994.

Greenbie, Marjorie Barstow. *Lincoln's Daughters of Mercy*, GP Putnam's Sons, New York, NY 1944.

Hamblen, Charles and Walter Powell, eds. *Connecticut Yankees At Gettysburg*. Kent State University Press, Kent, Ohio, 1993.

Harmon, Troy. *Lee's Real Plan At Gettysburg*, Stackpole Books, 2003.

Hill, Napoleon. *Think and Grow Rich*, Renaissance Books, 1960.

Holland, Mary A. Gardner. *Our Army Nurses*, B. Wilkins & Co., Boston, 1895.

Kowalis, Jeffrey J. and Loree. *Died at Gettysburg!*, Longstreet House, Highstown, NJ, 1998.

Leckie, Robert. *None Died In Vain: The Saga of the American Civil War*. HarperCollins, New York, 1990.

Peter, Laurence J. *The Peter Principle*, William Morrow & Co., 1969.

Pfanz, Harry W. *Gettysburg - The Second Day*, University of North Carolina Press, 1987.

Phipps, Michael. *"Come On, You Wolverines!"*, Farnsworth House Military Impressions, Gettysburg, PA, 1995.

Riley, Michael A. *"For God's Sake, Forward!"*, Farnsworth House, Gettysburg, PA, 1995.

Robertson, James I. *General A.P. Hill*. Random House, New York, 1987.

Rodenbough, Theo. *Uncle Sam's Medal of Honor*, G.P. Putnam's Sons, New York, 1886.

Rollins, Richard, ed. *Pickett's Charge: Eyewitness Accounts*, Rank and File Publications, Redondo Beach, CA, 1994.

Schneider, Richard. *Taps: Notes from a Nation's Heart*, William Morrow and Co., 2002.

Sears, Stephen W. *Gettysburg*, Houghton Mifflin Company, 2003.

Silliker, Ruth, ed. *The Rebel Yell & The Yankee Hurrah*, Down East Press, Camden, Maine, 1985.

Small, Cindy L. *The Jennie Wade Story*, Thomas Publications, Gettysburg, PA, 1991.

Southern Historical Society Papers, Vols. 6, 26.

Stewart, George. *Pickett's Charge*. Houghton Mifflin, Boston, 1959.

Symonds, Craig L. *American Heritage, History of the Battle of Gettysburg*, Byron Preiss Visual Publications, HarperCollins Publishers Inc., NY, 2001.

Trudeau, Noah Andre. *Gettysburg, A Testing of Courage*, HarperCollins, NY, 2002.

Trulock, Alice. *In The Hands of Providence*, North Carolina Press, Chapel Hill, NC, 1992.

United States War Department, *The War Of The Rebellion: A Compilation Of The Official Records of the Union and Confederate Armies*, 79 Vols. in 128 Parts (Washington DC Govt. Printing Office, 1880-1901). Series 1, Vol. 27, Parts 1 and 2, reissued as *The Civil War CD-ROM*, Guild Press of Indiana, Inc., 1997.

Useem, Michael. *The Leadership Moment*, Times Books, NY, 1998.

Wellman, Manly Wade. *Giant in Gray*, Morningside Books, 1996.

Wheeler, Richard. *Witness To Gettysburg*, Harper & Row, NY, 1987.

Wiggin, Lt. Francis. *Sixteenth Maine At Gettysburg*, War Papers, Maine MOLLUS, Vol. 4, Dec. 7, 1910.

Gettysburg Magazine volumes: No. 3, *Addendum to: The Supreme Event In Its Existence: The 140th N.Y. at Little Round Top*, Brian A. Bennett, March, 1996; No. 5, *A.P. Hill's Advance to Gettysburg*, Douglas Craig Haines, July, 1991; No 5, *Baptism of Fire...* Eric Campbell; No. 5, *The Death and Burials of General Richard Brooke Garnett*, Stephen Davis; No. 8, *The Hardtack Regiment In The Brickyard Fight*, Mark H. Dunkelman and Michael J. Winey, January, 1993; No. 8, *Pvt. Robert G Carter and the 22nd Massachusetts at Gettysburg*, Anthony J. Milano, January 1993; No. 13, *Over The Wall*, Roger Long, July 1995; No. 13, *A Meteorological And Astrological Chronology of the Gettysburg Campaign*, Thomas L. Elmore; No. 14, *Never Shirking A Duty Or Betraying A Trust*, James Durkin, January, 1996; No. 18, *The Second Wave Of Pickett's Charge*, Richard Rollins, Jan. 1998; No. 19, *"Give Them Another Volley, Boys": Briddle's Brigade Defends The Union Left on July 1, 1863*, Kevin O'Brien, July, 1998; No 19, *The Gettysburg Wounded and The "Flying Battery" Sisters*, James Durkin, July, 1998; No. 17, *Edward Porter Alexander, Confederate Cannoneer At Gettysburg*, Jay Jorgensen, July, 1997; No. 24, *JEB Stuart's Fateful Ride*, David L. Callahan, Jan 2001; No. 24, *"Fighting Alex" Hays At Gettysburg*, Wayne Mahood, January 2001; No. 26, *The Kilpatrick/Farnsworth Exchange*, Andie Custer, Jan 2003.

Civil War Times, August 1998, p. 88. Re: Orpheus Woodward.

Lee's Grand Strategy and Pickett's Charge, Richard Rollins, North and South Magazine, July 2002, pp. 76-84. Also by the same author, *Robert E. Lee and The Hand of God*, North & South, Jan. 2003, pp. 13-25.

The Knight of Romance, Andie Custer, Blue & Gray Magazine, Vol 22, Issue 2, pp. 6-23.

Philadelphia Times, *Storming Cemetery Hill*, Oct, 21, 1882, Thomas D. Houston.

Report to Fifth Wisconsin Association 1904, *The March of the Sixth Corps to Gettysburg*, by J.S. Anderson, contributed by James Johnson, 2nd Wisconsin Volunteer Infantry.

Poem

John Burns of Gettysburg, circa 1872 by Bret Harte (1836-1902).

Tapes

How To Stay Motivated, Zig Ziglar, Tape 1, Sides A and B.

Acknowledgements

I came to the writing of this book quite by accident. One of my sons came home with a history assignment from grade school and was required to write a report on one of twenty famous Americans. On the list were the obvious: Washington, Jefferson, Franklin, and Lincoln. But included on the list were the totally unexpected: Jimmy Hendrix and Janis Joplin, two high-profile, conspicuously amoral musicians who died from drug overdoses. I was quickly convinced that the history teacher surrendered all responsibility to instruct my son on why he ought to study the obvious. McHistory was making its debut in my town, but I wasn't buying. "Historical illiteracy is a threat to our national security," said columnist George Will, who came to this alarming but certain conclusion: "You cannot defend what you cannot define."

It took me no time to hit the libraries, the internet, and the keyboard. I sought to make history come alive with some zip and flare; I wanted my sons, and by extension, the reader to know that reading history can be profitable, even in the sense - brace yourself - of making money with it. I set out to write a book that would teach my sons how to succeed, but they had to see proof that within them is the power to influence people and their surroundings in order to achieve. I wanted to prove it by using an historical event that would breathe life into the event itself, citing ordinary people who succeeded in the middle of the most stressful moments in their lives. My sons could then appreciate history's screaming lessons that could do nothing more than lead them to pursue happiness two to three pages at a time.

Part of my energetic pursuit was finding reliable people to help me achieve my goal with this book. Michael Useem of the Wharton School of Business, and author of *The Leadership Moment*, was responsible and gracious for suggesting an overview of the battle and maps as context for the lessons. Paul Tusini was an adept editor who offered critical insights into business as well as provide honest and forthright advice on how to structure each story and its lessons. Antigoni Ladd's professional expertise in editing was a welcome contribution. My lifelong mentor, the late Oscar E. Remick, philosopher and theologian, provided unique observations about symbols, character and oaths, not to mention living a life fueled by a passion to see his students succeed. James Hogarth, West Point '77 and internationally recognized expert on electric vehicles, offered valuable recommendations on how to view military strategy as it pertains to business strategy. James Zack, national lecturer and advisor to business and industry, provided observations that were incorporated into several lessons. Doris Gagnon, retired head nurse of a Maine hospital staff, offered terrific suggestions on how to view the behavior of Gettysburg's nurses Sophrina Bucklin, Helen Gilson, Elmira Spencer and Carmilla O'Keefe. The late Richard Rollins, a maverick Civil War historian who found more facts under rocks no one else had yet turned over, provided many emails regarding his insights on Pickett's Charge, Generals Lee, Longstreet and Meade. In the same vein of originality was Gettysburg's highly regarded cavalry expert, Andie Custer, who was especially helpful with her myth-shattering research on Kilpatrick. David Ward, a direct descendant of Union colonel George Ward, was very accommodating in shedding light on the details of his great, great grandfather who fell on the second day. Historian Ben Maryiack provided his research on Bayard Wilkeson that could not be found elsewhere. Author Michael Drees offered his expert knowledge on George McFarland. One of Gettysburg's park rangers, Charles Teague, was a patient fact-checker. My sons John and Mark were able to offer a teenager's one-word review - "Cool!" - to the remarkable stories of teenagers like Tillie Pierce, Bayard Wilkeson and Robert Carter. Finally, my caring wife, Ann Marie, provided plenty of encouragement throughout the research and final writing of the manuscript.

Notes on a Discovery

Five years after I began researching this book, I made my sixth journey to Gettysburg, not as a historian in search of a new fact to uncover, but like most visitors to the National Park, as an American who stands in awe of what happened there. Each time I approach the outskirts of this small Pennsylvania town, I begin to realize that I am now entering the largest open-air sanctuary in America. All is very quiet as I attempt to grasp what surrounds me. Instead, it holds me firmly in its grasp revealing itself in a breezy calm, an uncommon stillness, as if to require the heart to stop for a moment of silence.

As I continued into the town, I made my usual stops to the common points of interest, but this trip held a surprise for me that I could never have imagined. Inside the National Cemetery, only yards from where Abraham Lincoln delivered his famous Address, I observed something extraordinary while walking among the graves of both known and unknown: I discovered a gravestone whose inscription was simple, which brought me to my knees and would eventually gift me a whole new meaning of Gettysburg:

D. Hemphill
Co E Regt 72

Page Index of Lessons by Category

Note to the reader

As stated in the Introduction, I haven't thought of all the stories from Gettysburg that could be included in this book. So please contact me by email and tell me whose story you would tell and what lessons you think the reader can learn that have *not* already been stated. If your story and its Gettysburg Lessons ought to be included in the next edition, I'll include them and credit you as the source.

Paul Lloyd Hemphill
ura@leadertoo.com

About The Author

Sketched here as "Lincoln's General," the author appears in period uniform to speak to audiences about his favorite topic: leadership.

Frustrated with how his children were learning history in high school, he decided to write a book that taught how an historical event could be relevant to his sons' lives. He set out to prove that reading history can be a motivational experience that teaches important life-lessons that are rewarding both intellectually and emotionally, thereby making history come alive.

After college, his most memorable experience was serving in Vietnam with the 25th Infantry Division as a chaplain's assistant, where he was awarded the Bronze Star and the Vietnamese Cross of Gallantry. Later he came close to failing in a business venture in 1985, and subsequently worked with the day-to-day pressures of being self-employed for twelve years. In each of these stressful environments, he was able to overcome numerous obstacles, and in 1997 achieved national recognition from the National Association for the Self-Employed for reaching his personal and professional goals.

While reading about the battle of Gettysburg in the late 1990s, he discovered that ordinary people - over one hundred and fifty years ago - performed in the same manner as he did under stress. With his desire to convince Americans that reading their history is a profitable activity, the author uses it here to convince us of our innate ability to lead and succeed. That is why honoring heroes, says the author, is simply recognizing the leadership ability we all possess.

He has been a college admissions coach and marketer for more than 10 years, and resides in Norfolk, Massachusetts with his wife, Ann Marie.